LEITCH RIT

A J O U R N E Y

TO

ST. PETERSBURG AND MOSCOW

THROUGH

C O U R L A N D A N D L I V O N I A

Elibron Classics
www.elibron.com

Elibron Classics series.

© 2005 Adamant Media Corporation.

ISBN 1-4021-7570-1 (paperback)
ISBN 1-4021-1250-5 (hardcover)

This Elibron Classics Replica Edition is an unabridged facsimile
of the edition published in 1836 by Longman, Rees, Orme, Brown,
Green, and Longman, London.

HEATH'S
PICTURESQUE ANNUAL,
FOR 1836.
St. Petersburg and Moscow.

Tower of the Nikolskoi Church St Petersburg

From Drawings by
ALFRED GEORGE VICKERS, ESQ.

LONDON, PUBLISHED FOR THE PROPRIETOR BY LONGMAN & Cº. PATERNOSTER ROW,
RITTNER & Cº. PARIS & ASHER BERLIN.

A JOURNEY

TO

ST. PETERSBURG AND MOSCOW

THROUGH

COURLAND AND LIVONIA.

BY

LEITCH RITCHIE, Esq.

AUTHOR OF "TURNER'S ANNUAL TOUR," "SCHINDERHANNES," &c.

WITH

TWENTY-FIVE SPLENDID ENGRAVINGS,

BY THE FIRST ARTISTS.

AFTER DRAWINGS,

BY A. G. VICKERS, Esq.

LONDON:

LONGMAN, REES, ORME, BROWN, GREEN, AND LONGMAN.

PARIS: RITTNER AND GOUPILL. BERLIN: A. ASHER.

1836.

LONDON :

PRINTED BY J. HADDON AND CO., DOCTORS' COMMONS.

ADVERTISEMENT.

———

THE former volumes of the Picturesque
Annual, although aspiring to a permanent place
in the library, were yet written with some reference to the character of drawing-room table
books stamped upon them by their gorgeous
binding and exquisite engravings. When the
author, however, undertook to travel in RUSSIA,
—a country about which so many conflicting
opinions have been published,—he thought he
would best consult the advantage of the public
by making his book a work entirely of information, and allowing whatever amusement it
might contain to depend upon the nature of
the facts communicated.

It was with this idea he set out upon the journey, and he soon found reason to congratulate himself upon his decision. He has not indulged either in theory or controversy. He has given a plain account of what he saw with his own eyes, and heard with his own ears; and however much the narrative may in some parts be condemned by former travellers and their admirers, he is conscious that it will one day receive credit for its truth.

The critical reader is requested to bear in mind the manifest inadequacy of the space afforded by this little volume. The author hopes very soon to have leisure to make use of the rest of his materials.

CONTENTS.

ENGRAVINGS,

FROM DRAWINGS BY ALFRED GEORGE VICKERS, ESQ.

ERRATUM.

The engraving at page 136 is a view of the Alexandrine Column, and not of the ceremony of its coronation, as is there stated. The author referred by mistake to another of the artist's drawings, which is not yet published.

A JOURNEY

TO

ST. PETERSBURG AND MOSCOW.

CHAPTER I.

Departure from Memel—frontiers of Prussia on the Baltic—
entrance into Russia—douane—reflections preliminary to
the inquiries that are to follow—Russian inns—change of
climate—living on the road—amusements—scenery—peasantry—arrival at Mittau and detention there by the governor—the town and its inhabitants—Jew-smugglers—beards
and costumes—departure.

In the middle of April, 1835, I set out from
Memel, the last frontier town of Prussia on the
Baltic, with the intention of visiting St. Petersburg
and Moscow, and returning to England by the way
of Warsaw, Berlin, and Hamburg.

At St. Petersburg I hoped to become acquainted
with Modern Russia, and to be enabled to form some
idea of the real progress of her civilization, in so far
at least, as this is indicated in the manners of the

B

people; at Moscow, in the heretofore capital of the Tsars, I should find myself in the very heart of the ancient empire, where the tribes and nations of the distant dependencies still resort as to a common centre; and in Poland an opportunity would present itself of studying the character of the most interesting of the conquered provinces, the preservation of which costs more in blood, and tears, and money than a whole continent is worth.

My carriage, the best I could obtain for hire in Memel, resembled a diligence, which, having fallen into superannuation and decay, had been cut down for private use; and this machine was drawn by three horses abreast, the leader being very well worthy of his dignity, by nearly two feet of advantage over the others in point of stature. The driver was a tall, hale, ruddy old man, with a physiognomy strongly expressive of the quiet good humour of the Prussians. Like the postillions of his country, he rarely used his whip, preferring to yield rather than resort to violence; and as rarely did he give himself the trouble either of remonstrating or encouraging by words. In England this mode of government could not exist, for there the horses are only permitted to see straight forward; and, to comprehend their master behind, they must be made both to hear and feel. In Prussia their eyes are uncovered, and it is curious to observe the anxious attention with which they watch the motions of the, to them, harmless whip.

The road, soon after leaving the town, conducted us into a wilderness of sand and water, where it seemed, by the wheel tracts, that each carriage was in the habit of choosing its own way. Having traversed Prussia in its greatest length my eyes were not unaccustomed to scenery of the kind; but I question whether even in the deserts of Brandenburg, in the midst of which stands the capital—like a city transported thither by enchantment from the habitable world—there can any thing be seen more dreary and desolate.

We at length reached a solitary habitation, apparently a toll-house. The bar, painted with the royal colours, black and white, was raised. No one appeared either to exact dues, or to question the passerby as to his whereabout; but the coachman stopped at the door, and took in my passport. In a minute or two he returned and we resumed our journey, and I found that I had passed through one of the entrance or exit gates of Prussia.

The desert became still more desolate, and the wind began to moan with that strange unearthly sound which it has in lonely places, over tracts of snow or sand. To the left, the wilderness was bound in by the distant Baltic as with a girdle, only distinguishable from the sky, with which it mingled, by its deeper blue. Every where else fields of sand and morass extended to the verge of the horizon. This apparently was a neutral ground between the two countries; and it was with no small degree of curiosity that I awaited my introduction into Russia.

The gate at length appeared, and its stripes of

black and white, the former colour edged with red, so nearly resembled those of Prussia that I began to fancy I had been premature. The next moment, however, the ring of arms upon the pavement re-assured me. As the carriage entered, it was stopped by Cossacks with fixed bayonets; and one mounting behind, I was thus driven like a prisoner of state, to the douane.

The door of this house was guarded by armed sentinels, and in a room opening into the one where my luggage was examined, a Cossack stood, like a wooden figure, with fixed bayonet. The examining officers were in uniform, and wore swords; but they were not otherwise different from their brethren of England or France, than by a gentlemanly courtesy, which in those countries appears to be considered out of the way of the profession. They exhibited none of the vulture-like eagerness about trifles which renders the customhouse even of London at once vexatious and ridiculous; and so far from turning over my things like Jew-clothesmen, they were only anxious to prevent the attendants from disturbing their arrangement.* I must add that of the few books I had, only one was opened.

My passport, however, was an affair not so easily managed. The questions they put were innumer-

---

* On this subject every traveller differs, not only from others but from himself. The conduct of the customhouse officers varies at every port and with every change of individuals; and it may be well to remark that the last time I visited London (since writing the text) I had nothing whatever to complain of.

able, and the entries made in consequence by the clerk, would have sufficed for a memoir. At length all was over; and willingly granting the request made openly by the attendants for a small gratuity, I pursued my journey, marvelling not a little at the complaints made by some former travellers of the hardships and indignities they had endured from the frontier police of Russia.

I was not destined, however, to escape with absolute ease myself. At a distance of two or three hundred yards, at the entrance of a small village, we were again stopped by soldiers with fixed bayonets, and my passport again demanded. I confess I gave it with reluctance, being unable to conceive what purpose all this could serve; and when one of them coolly stepped into the carriage, and desired me to open my portmanteau for the second time, it was with a very bad grace indeed I obeyed. But when the fellow, after putting me to this unnecessary, and as I was convinced, unlawful trouble, demanded money, my trifling stock of patience failed me all on a sudden, and I ordered the coachman to drive on. The man hesitated, and looked, or affected to look alarmed, and the soldiers persisted more clamourously; but when I attempted to leap out of the carriage in order to return to the douane to complain, they raised the siege at once, and their curses, "not loud but deep," mingled with the rattle of the wheels as we drove on. I told this anecdote afterwards to the Chief of the Secret Police at St. Petersburg, and perhaps the nuisance exists no more; but in case it should still continue, I now relate the circumstance for the benefit of quietly disposed travellers. These persons should throw the beggarly ruffians a small silver coin on their passport being demanded, and desire their coachman to proceed.

We speedily entered a forest, in which we wandered the whole day, and where I had nothing more amusing than my own reflections to beguile the time. These were naturally occupied with the country I had entered. It seemed to me that I was already able to account for the conflicting statements even of the most recent travellers, and that at my first step into Russia, I had seen both sides of the medal. It would be illiberal and unbecoming to charge some of my predecessors with prejudice; for this, when applied to a traveller—to one who sees the world in its different forms, and mankind in their different phases, amounts to a charge of absolute stupidity; but surely they have not weighed with due attention the remarkable circumstances in which this very remarkable nation has been placed.

M. Bachoutsky, a Russian author, gives himself the trouble of quoting an inquiry into the relative degree of civilization of the great nations of Europe at recent periods—but this is all in vain. The insulated facts from which he would reason, can no more be taken as evidences of the character of a people, than a stone as a sample of a building. No sophistry can conceal the truth that a century ago the old nations of Europe were not greatly different, in the moral features of civilization, from what they are now, and that at the same period the Russians were in a state of the darkest barbarism. The boiars lived in their chateaux, whether at Moscow or in the provinces, plunged in all the ignorance of the feudal age. Their character was not elevated by a single trait even of that fantastic species of refinement which forms the poetical charm of the times of chivalry. Their women were at the same time secluded like Eastern slaves, and insulted, beaten, and occasionally murdered with impunity, like the wives of savages. Their religion was half paganism, or more than half; and Panitsa, the Venus of the heathen, jostled the Virgin Mary even in the temples.

Such was the chaos in which the elements of a great people were plunged when the genius of Peter the Great first " moved upon the face of the waters." This man, rude in his manners, fierce in his passions, and vulgar in his tastes and habits, was in some respects no bad representative of his country; but in the finer part of his nature, he was one of those intellectual giants who appear at long intervals among meaner men, like a comet among the stars. Nay, his very rudeness rendered him the better tamer of a rude people. No tricks of refinement, no Machiavellian cunning would have had any effect in a case like this. Peter carried his purposes into execution by the strong hand. He *compelled* his subjects to assume the manners, well knowing that this would bring about in time the reality, of civilization ; and

rushing in upon the old boiar in his native woods,
he shaved his beard by main force,

"And dragged the struggling savage into day."

That absolute power is in itself a prodigious evil
no one can deny, but in this case it was productive
of positive good.   At any rate, when the creations of
absolute power are beneficial to the people, they are
necessarily destructive of itself—a fact which will
probably receive some illustration in the course of this
work.   The successors of Peter, however, trod stea-
dily in the same path.   In particular his wife,
Catherine I., the licentious Catherine II., the late
emperor Alexander, all pursued, and his present
majesty still pursues, the wise plans of their great
prototype.   What have they effected?   Of that I
hope to obtain some idea in the course of my tour;
but it is necessary, on setting out, to ascertain the
time afforded for the ripening of these gigantic plans,
and for the execution of their multitudinous details.

It is true that the Emperor Alexis laid the first
step, the vantage ground, from which his son was
one day to take his magnificent flight; but with
Peter himself commenced the real civilization of the
Russians.   Since his death there have elapsed one
hundred and ten years; but of these only *seventy*
have been occupied by the above-mentioned princes,
while the remainder is divided among the comparatively unproductive reigns of Peter II., Anne,
Ivan, Elizabeth, Peter III., and the unhappy Paul.

We thus arrive at the true data on which to proceed, and the only one which will enable the traveller to form a correct estimate of the character of
the Russian nation, and of the present condition and
prospects of the country. With these data in his
mind, the stranger will either exclaim conscien-
tiously against the ignorance and stupidity of the
people in having effected so little; or he will inquire
in astonishment, how they could have done so much
in so short a period. What a pity it is that philosophers so rarely travel ; or, at least, in sending us
of the staff and wallet to fetch materials, that they
do not lend us their own spectacles !

About mid-day we halted for dinner at an inn
in the middle of the forest. The inns on this road
are all of the same construction; and, although very
unlike such places in France or England, are by no
means uncomfortable. The coachman knocks at an
immense door, and horses, carriage, and all, are
driven into the house. The traveller finds himself
in a vast oblong hall, surrounded by the equipages
of other travellers, and at the further end of which
there is another door for his exit. The postillions
are mending their tackle, the horses feeding, and
flights of fowls fluttering and screaming around as
they contest with one another the scattered grains
of corn. Confused by the noise and darkness visible
of the place, he is guided by his coachman to a side
door, which opens into the portion of the house
destined for the reception of two-legged guests; and
here he finds a suite, generally of three or four large

rooms, in any one of which he may establish himself for his meal.

The furniture of these rooms, although cheap, is extremely handsome; the chairs and tables being made of birch brilliantly polished, and, when new, bearing a strong resemblance to satin-wood. The walls are covered with bad prints, chiefly English, and the window-sills with flowering plants, even in the depth of winter. During that season, and, indeed, for eight months of the year, every apartment is a true hot-house, the atmosphere being kept up to a certain high temperature by stoves. The windows are double—that is to say, there are two glazed window-frames in each aperture, a single pane of which is made to open, so as to render a change of atmosphere in the room at least possible; while every other joint or seam is carefully pasted over with paper. In each apartment, it must be added, there are three or four beds; but these, being extremely narrow, take up no more room than a sofa, as it is not the custom here for the husband and wife to occupy the same couch.

My dinner consisted of a white soup, made of milk, butter, vegetables, and *sucking pig*, together with a portion of roasted turkey. The meal upon the whole, notwithstanding the blackness and sourness of the bread, was very acceptable to a hungry traveller: but, alas! with me it was "toujours perdrix!"—for five consecutive days I could get nothing else to eat than white soup and roasted turkey.

At the inn where I slept I found a clean and comfortable bed, although the chambermaid had the atrocity almost to insist upon my sleeping in one close to the hot stove ; and I was lulled to sleep by the songs of a large company of peasants assembled in the kitchen. Some of them sung in parts, while the others contributed the chorus. The music was in general simple and mournful, and many of the voices were singularly sweet.

In the morning as we resumed our journey, I felt very sensibly that I had been travelling northward for some weeks. When I left Paris the weather was almost disagreeably warm ; while here, the pools by the road side were covered with ice, and the trees clothed in their winter finery of hoar-frost. As the beams of the early sun slanted through the branches, the effect was the most beautiful imaginable. The fable of the Magician's garden seemed to be realized, for every leaf was hung with sapphires, rubies, and emeralds. The trees were chiefly pines, with here and there a few birches, gleaming with a spectral whiteness through the mysterious gloom ; and below there was almost always an underwood of juniper, and a rich green carpet of *blaeberry bushes*.

We at length emerged from this seemingly interminable forest, and the view opened suddenly, disclosing numerous farmsteads and cottages scattered over the face of rather a picturesque country. The road led across a rapid stream, somewhat violent in winter, if one may judge by the strength of the breakwaters. These did not form a part of the bridge; but, as is customary in Russia, were constructed at a distance of a good many feet. This description of view was closed by the first country seat I had seen since passing the frontiers. The ground story of the building was white, and the upper red, but notwithstanding, the effect was far from being disagreeable. Beyond this, the scene changed into a most desolate heath, interspersed with small pools, with woods and hills in the distance.

At the inn where we dined this day the room was hung with living ivy, festooned with great regularity. It grew in little pots placed on the sills of the numerous windows. Having desired to taste at dinner some London porter of which the hostess boasted, it was set before me with sugar and a spoon; and, seeing me reject these appendages, the good woman lingered in the room with evident curiosity to watch how the nasty foreigner could otherwise swallow such a potion. This mode of serving English porter I afterwards found to be customary even in the larger towns.

The scenery now improved every step we advanced till it became absolutely picturesque, exhibiting all the varieties of hill and valley, wood and lake, with here and there patches of cultivated ground. At every house we passed there was one unfailing appendage—a swing; and the peasantry might be correctly described as being divided into two classes, those who were swinging, and those who were waiting for a swing. I observed a mother passing by with her child at her breast eye long-ingly the tempting apparatus. At that moment the seat became vacant, and, giving the baby to another to hold, she ran to indulge herself in a swing. The girl who waited at dinner, when standing by the window, saw the swing unoccupied; and, pretending to be called, immediately left the room. I saw her dart across the road, and into the swing; and, when she had made three or four aerial courses, she came back satisfied. The men swing standing upon the seat, sometimes several at a time; the women in a sitting posture.

This machine is occasionally made of hewn wood, in the form of a gallows; but, in general, it consists of a branch of a tree fastened transversely between two pines near the top, with two slender trees hanging down from it instead of ropes, connected at the bottom by what serves for the seat. Neither hemp nor iron enters into the construction, the fastenings being all of tough roots and lichens.

The next day the scenery was strangely diversi-fied, now exhibiting a desert of sand, and now a rich and picturesque country. We passed another rapid stream, by a flying bridge, leaving behind a village and château near the bank. As yet the Russian villages consisted merely of isolated dwell-ings, widely scattered, without any attempt at a general plan; arising, as it would seem, partly from the cheapness of land, and partly from the difficulty of finding an area of productive ground sufficiently large for the whole community. In a picturesque spot like this they are always a deformity. Their white walls and fiery red roofs give them the appearance of the houses we see in a child's picture-book. Neither are the rural churches in this part of the country very poetical objects. They are surmounted by a short, sturdy, peremptory-looking cone, sheathed with tin or copper; and are usually seen in isolated situations, where they serve as a common rendezvous for several villages. Glens, and woods, and vales, now opened and shut around us as we rolled past, with swelling hills in the distance, or dark forests bounding the horizon.

The peasants as yet were still in European costume. They wore a kind of tunic, chiefly of blue or grey cloth, and not unlike an English frock coat. Sometimes this was lined with sheep fur. The women exhibited little peculiarity in dress, and were inferior to the men in personal appearance. The men appear fond of the inn kitchen, answering to the tap-room of London; but I did not observe a single instance of intoxication. At the bar, which is generally a little room adjoining the kitchen, while waiting to be served, they stood round the landlord, hat in hand, exchanging their remarks only in a whisper. The publicans here appear to be personages of great importance, or else the peasants are very far down indeed in the scale of being. When making my way the next evening through the kitchen, ushered by a pretty young creature, the daughter of the landlord, she pushed through the crowd as if it consisted of cattle,

thrusting her customers aside with a gesture of
angry contempt. I have repeatedly observed the
same thing, however, in Ireland. I have repeatedly
seen a merchant's clerk, when tormented by the
voices of the peasants who had come to be settled
with for the butter they had sold him in the market,
snatch up a stick, leap across the counter, and drive
them out with blows, like a herd of oxen.

In the inn I allude to, I met, for the first time
in this country, with a stray Englishman. I could
not tell what he was, nor whither he was going, nor
do I think he knew himself. He was a citizen of
the world, but unacquainted with the individual
countries which compose it. He spoke all lan-
guages with equal fluency, and all equally badly ;
now snuffling French, now expectorating German,
and now lubricating his mouth with Italian as one
greases a coach-wheel. If this is what we English
gain by travelling, we had better stay at home.
The next morning the scenery was still picturesque,
with spaces of waste land between. We passed a
ruined castle to the right, apparently of no great
antiquity, about which I could learn nothing; and
soon after arrived at Mittau, the capital of Courland.

As it was my intention to remain only a few
hours in this little city, I left the carriage at the
inn, and went to the police to get my passport
viséd. Some detention occurred owing to the principal functionary being *asleep;* but, at length, he
condescended to awake, and I learnt that I must

here give up my old passport, and obtain a new one.
This did not surprise me, being accustomed to see
the same kind of foolish and clumsy machinery in
operation at Calais, for the purpose of putting a
couple of francs into the pockets of the King of the
French; and in due time all was arranged, and I
was sent with a messenger to the Chancellerie of the
Governor. At the chancellerie I was desired to call
the next day.

This was "too bad." I travelled with a passport
from the English government, signed by all the
ambassadors and other competent functionaries of
Russia I had met on my way; and in this dirty
little town I was now to be laid hold of like a male-
factor, and imprisoned in it for a day and a night! I
immediately waited upon the Governor to represent
my case. He at first appeared unwilling to listen;
but I insisted doggedly that my horses were waiting, and that I had at least a right to know of what
crime I was suspected, in order to justify my detention. The governor appeared embarrassed, but at
length vented his displeasure in some angry excla-
mations against his clerks, to whom he sent to know
the cause of their conduct, retiring in the meantime
himself into the next room. In a few minutes he
re-entered, and with many polite apologies informed
me, that to-day it was a *holiday* in his chancellerie,
and that, therefore, I must absolutely remain in the
town till next morning. This holiday, I afterwards
learnt, takes place invariably on the arrival of a
stranger at Mittau, even when he presents himself

at the château early in the morning: but it is only justice to the present governor to say that he has made himself obnoxious to the townspeople by the reformation of various other abuses, introduced, or protected, by his predecessor.

Disorders, as annoying as the above, are observable in all the great continental governments, with one exception. In Prussia they are fully sensible of the inestimable value of Public Opinion; and, perhaps, to this cause alone may be attributed the enduring tranquillity of a country where the citizen-soldiers are superior, both in numbers and military experience, to the standing army.

Mittau is built of wood, with the exception of the governor's château, which is a large square building, with a good deal of the air of a royal palace. This, it will be recollected, was for some time the asylum of Louis XVIII. Some of the other houses are sufficiently handsome, and several of the streets clean and genteel-looking. The shop doors are usually decorated with representations of the articles sold, even the minutest,—such as pins and needles, —and all very accurately executed. I was in particular amused by the painting on a barber's shop which exhibited the operation performed within, in figures nearly as large as life. The zeal of the operator, and the heroic resignation of the unhappy shavee, are depicted with a spirit that is truly edifying. These pictures are on the outer doors, which fold back against the wall. The inner, which are partly glazed, open into the shop.

The principal inhabitants of Mittau are noble families of small incomes, whose numerous equipages give an aristocratic air to the place. These are attracted hither, I presume, by the extreme cheapness of the necessaries, and some of the luxuries, of life. Meat is only two pence an English pound; a pair of chickens may be bought for eight pence; a turkey, in high condition, for sixteen pence; and a large brown loaf, weighing between three and four pounds, costs only a penny. Their servants, therefore, can be cheaply supported; and, as the wages of a man are seldom higher than six pounds a year, they may easily gratify the national propensity for the display of a numerous retinue. As for articles of foreign produce, they are supplied at comparatively little cost, by Jew-smugglers. The town absolutely swarms with these desperadoes; and, even in the courts of gentlemen's houses, if there is a nook at all capable of affording shelter, you see a Hebrew family nestling like a colony of mice. They are, of course, tolerated by the nobles, who by their means are able to enjoy various little luxuries, which their pride would otherwise demand in vain of their poverty: but the government, whose interest is quite on the other side, has sometimes the cruelty to send them in whole gangs to Siberia. Money, however, like Pierre's mistress, is a Jew's religion; and the instances of martyrdom they witness around them only serve to animate their zeal.

Almost all the lower classes wear their beards

uncut, and often untrimmed. These appendages, however must not be judged of by the Jewish beards we see in London; for a London Jew so adorned always looks filthy and unapproachable. In Russia they are absolutely ornamental; and the peasants more especially derive from them a certain manliness of air which is highly interesting. I saw at Mittau some truly noble-looking figures, tall and athletic, with uncovered heads, and their magnificent beards appearing in well-defined relief against their bare necks. The men were usually clothed in a sheepskin tunic, with the wool inside, and boots reaching to the knees. The women are good-looking, not to say handsome; and the Jewesses, with a shawl-turban round their head, look picturesque and oriental.

The next day I was detained two hours at the governor's chancellerie; but, at length, being permitted to depart, we set out for Riga, where my engagement with the coachman and his horses was to terminate; and where we arrived after a few hours' ride through a flat, uninteresting country. This is, upon the whole, the worst avenue into Russia that could be chosen, for there is really little to be seen. I would advise travellers, even from France, to proceed to Lubeck, and take a passage in the steam vessel to Riga.

CHAPTER II.

Arrival at Riga—idea of a Russo-Greek church—description
of the town—Saint Hercules—market scene—floating
houses on the Dwina—Hotels of Riga—tyranny of the
custom-house.

WHEN we arrived at the banks of the Dwina, we
found that the bridge, taken to pieces, as is customary in autumn, was not yet replaced, and we
prepared to cross the river in a ferry boat. The
scene was filled with animation. Numerous barges
were about to sail at the same instant, and many
more were crossing and re-crossing in all directions.
On the other side a double or treble row of ships
lined the water's edge for a considerable distance;
and beyond these, the fortified mounds, the dark roofs
and spires and domes of the capital of Livonia, gave
an imposing finish to the picture.

Riga is so closely compressed within its earthen
walls that the business transacted in the narrow and

confined streets appears to be still greater than it really is. The houses of these streets, however, are in general well built, and some of them even handsome. The town appears in its best aspect when entered through the citadel; its tapering spires and small domes being then seen richly grouped together. In the citadel itself the church is a very elegant little building, with a spire of the most beautiful proportions; and although a part of this, as well as the roof, is painted green, the effect is by no means unpleasing. In the interior, however, the space is so small, that the profusion of gold, silver, and paintings, thickly interspersed with lighted candles, gives it the appearance of a show-box.

It was here I saw for the first time, the rites of the Russo-Greek worship; and in this little temple the traveller will find an epitome of every thing remarkable in the national church. I do not mean to encroach upon my small space with descriptions of ceremonies so often described already; but I may take this opportunity, in order to avoid the necessity of explanation afterwards, of giving a general idea of the place.

The only seats in a Russian church are a line of benches which runs along the walls of the nave; and sometimes, in the middle, an article resembling one of those huge, square stools that are occasionally placed in our drawing rooms, like a bale of dry-goods in a warehouse. The stage, as it may be termed, is ascended by two or three steps; and the drop-scene behind called the Ikonastas, representing the curtain of the temple of Solomon, is a partition, sometimes ascending to the vault, with folding doors in the middle; and the form of this species of screen is different in almost every church. Sometimes it is altogether impervious to the eye; sometimes it is made of richly ornamented rail-work, through which a glimpse of the interior may be caught; and sometimes (as in the present case) there is a window at either side, through which you see the Holy Table covered with vases, candlesticks, and reliquaries, like the counter of an or-moulu shop. The screen is thickly studded with portraits of the saints richly framed, and in general the drapery of these figures is formed of gilded metal, so that only the faces and hands are seen.

A great part of the service is performed before the Holy Doors are opened, but, at a signal, these fly open, and the worshipper beholds the sanctuary, which the foot of *woman* must not profane (as if heaven could be desecrated by the presence of angels!) with the Holy Table surmounted by a canopy, from which a *peristerium*, or dove, is suspended, the symbol of the Holy Ghost. Through clouds of incense, the ministering priests are seen flitting slowly about, or preparing the mystic elements speedily to be enchanted into the true body and blood of Christ. Behind the altar is the High Place, the seat of the bishop, and where none but he may presume to sit. On the left hand is the *prothesis*, or table on which the Bread and Wine are made ready for the sacrifice; and at the right hand a place which serves for the vestry. The service is performed in a kind of recitative, and in the ancient Slavonian language, which the modern Russians only imperfectly understand; and this is interspersed with singing, the only music permitted. The people in the meantime perform their parts in the ceremony by bowing the head and body, prostrating themselves upon the ground, and touching the pavement with their foreheads. This is usually executed in a very graceful manner, especially by the women; who study the attitude as zealously as the fair devotees of the Anglican church do theirs in fulfilling literally the figurative prophecy of Scripture, " At the name of Jesus every knee shall bow."

On crossing the drawbridge of the citadel, in order to enter the town, you pass a small Catholic church to the right, and on the left two German churches; in one of which the organ is among the most beautiful I have ever seen. The beadle told me, with great pride, that it was considered to be the handsomest in all the Russias. The streets in the neighbourhood are, as elsewhere, narrow, but many of the houses are handsome, and built of stone. The other quarters of the town are far inferior; but what renders Riga almost insupportable is the state of the pavement. There is, indeed, a sort of trottoir paved with bricks, but this is so narrow, and so much interrupted by the steps of the houses, as to be nearly useless. As for the carriage way, I cannot give a better account of it than in the words of a little Scottish boy whom I passed as he was limping along. " Od !" said he, soliloquizing between his set teeth, "the folks here dinna ken how to causey ; they put the wrang end of the stanes uppermost !"

The suburbs of Riga are much more extensive than the town ; and the streets there are almost invariably wide and good. They are besides more Russian than the space within the walls, where the principal inhabitants and shopkeepers are German. On going out of one of the gates into the suburb called by the English the Foretown, I saw a crowd of persons crossing and prostrating themselves before an immense wooden statue resembling a Hercules with an infant on his shoulder. This modern god, they told me, was one of the popular heroes of the place ; who, when the town was in the hands of enemies, entered the gate in the disguise of a beggar, and held it open by main force till his companions followed.* The country people are perhaps little to blame in mistaking him for a saint ; but it shows how little they understand the puerile quibble of the Greek church, which compounds between idolatry and the second commandment by permitting the worship of pictures, and forbidding that of " graven images." Even in the temples themselves, however, this law is sometimes broken. In the Convent of the Miracles at Moscow, there is a bass-relief representing the Crucifixion engraved in wood, with a lamp burning before it, and in the Ivan-Velikoi in

---

* Since writing the above I have seen in the Cathedral of Lubeck a painting representing this " Hercules," who is there called Saint Christopher ! I forget the legend attached to it.

the same city there is a wooden statue of Saint Nicolas.

The daily market of Riga is held on the quay, and presents a very amusing and animated scene. Vegetables seem to be abundant; and in particular the asparagus is the finest I ever tasted. Live fish are brought in large tubs, as at Leipsig, and some other places in Germany. Sour cream, however, is the staple commodity, being an article used in almost every culinary preparation without exception. Soups, sauces, gravies, all derive a new richness from this auxiliary; and in particular the small peas, of which the Russians are so fond, could not be dressed without it. Among the fruits there were great quantities of cranberries, preserved fresh throughout the year, and used for juice, as well as for a summer drink that is said to be very agreeable. Blaeberries also are here in the proper season, and afford materials for jelly. They are larger than ours on the Scottish hills, and of a superior flavour. Bread and meat are about half the London price; but other articles, at least at this time of the year, present no remarkable difference. One part of the quay is occupied by a large open shed which serves for a café for the market people; who resort thither to drink quass, and eat great quantities of a very small kind of fish.

While ascending the river by the quay, I saw, beyond the termination of the line of ships, a number of smooth oblong eminences, resembling the sand hills near the entrance of the harbour at Memel.

These, on nearer approach, proved to be the barges which descend the Dwina every year from the interior of the country. Their burthen is usually about three hundred tons, and their construction as rude as possible. An immense oblong mound rises from the vessel, filling nearly her whole area, with the exception of a gangway running round, and a space at the bow and stern for working the ship. This mound is a vast warehouse, containing also the dwelling-house of the mariners, provided with a door and glazed windows; and being covered with Russian matting (made of the bark of the Linden tree) it looks at a little distance exactly like a sand hill. The small boats are real canoes, being made of nothing more than a hollow tree, with a broad pine plank at each side for the gunwale.

The men were picturesque figures, in their sheep-skin frocks, and gaily coloured shirts, worn over their small clothes. Instead of the long boots which are common among the Russians residing in towns, their legs were covered with pieces of linen cloth bandaged round with twine, or anything else that came to hand. Their shoes were made of matting, like the coverings of their wooden houses, and their hats of white coarse felt of all possible shapes. These persons work for some time at the roads or in the harbour, like the Irish in their incursions into England; and they may afterwards be seen in gangs trudging it back to their villages, with their staves thrust through a large black loaf hanging over their shoulder, and an earthen pot dangling at their waist.

As for the vessels and the wooden houses, they return no more. When the cargo is sold they are broken up for firewood, or to assist in the construction of cottages. Sometimes, in fact, these simple edifices are transported bodily into the neighbouring country; and the Livonian peasant inhabits a dwelling built in the interior of Poland.

There are two large hotels at Riga, the St. Petersburg and the London, but they are both abominably filthy. A lodging-house, however, has been lately established by a little Scottish widow—a kind of modern Meg Dods—where travellers will find themselves very comfortably situated. The house, which is called the King's Arms, is in a narrow street behind the quay; but in the interior it is one of the handsomest in the town. As yet it is chiefly frequented by ship masters, and the English merchants of the place hold there one of their clubs; but, for the benefit of my brother travellers, I advised the kind-hearted and attentive landlady to convert it into a general hotel.

Having given due honour to the frontier douane at which I was myself examined, I have now the less reluctance in representing the hardships and indignities to which British subjects are exposed, on their arrival by sea at Riga. This sort of discrepancy will be frequently observed throughout the volume. I have no system to uphold, and no design but to relate faithfully what I know. I honestly believe that the progress already made, and now making, by the Russians in civilization is without a

parallel in the history of nations; but at the same
time that progress has by no means been equal
throughout their institutions.

The examination of vessels on their arrival at a
foreign port must necessarily be strict; but here it
seems to be a part of the officers' duty to insult
as well as search. After rummaging a flour sack,
for instance, these fellows will thrust their hands,
without even shaking them, into the captain's wardrobe. His person is scrupulously examined, and
even after leaving the ship, he is liable to be stopped
in the street by any vagabond in the service. The
shame and indignation which many of these persons
expressed in conversation with me on the subject,
contrasts finely with the tranquil servility of our
government. One man never goes on shore without
having a ship boy walking behind him to take off his
master's hat in the streets when the custom-house
myrmidons command it. Another refused to perform
this operation, and desired the officer to do it himself. He was taken to the douane, and detained
there three hours before the affair could be accom-
modated. They are frequently stopped, while
making purchases in the market, and their pockets
publicly searched. The same stupidity of vigilance continues after the cargo has been discharged,
and a new one is taking in; and even then the
captain is prohibited from receiving visitors on board
his own ship. All this, it seems, must be passed
over, because it is "the custom of the country"—
and yet, in our embassies to really barbarous nations,

we are nothing loath to sacrifice life and treasure on a point of etiquette. Does the difference arise from the nations alluded to being *mere* barbarians, without weight in the scale of nations,—or from the circumstance of the envoy representing the Sovereign, while the traders represent merely the People of England?

If, after all, our government is really ignorant of the pitiful position in which the nation stands in Russia, I hope some public-spirited member of parliament will take occasion to move for a list of the salaries and duties of the British consuls in that country.*

---

* Some shipmasters, it seems, were detected in smuggling in their hats. The opportunity for this could only have arisen from the want of vigilance of the officers on board. When such a thing takes place, flog *both* parties and welcome, but do not insult a whole nation.

CHAPTER III.

NOTWITHSTANDING the constant intercourse between Riga and St. Petersburg, the diligence goes only once a week. It is, therefore, always full ; and as, at this season more especially, owing to the bad state of the roads, it is a mode of conveyance chosen even by those who usually travel in their own carriages, the stranger should not lose a moment in securing his seat.

I was fortunate in my fellow-travellers. Among the rest, we had the pastor Saraë, a Lutheran priest of Moldavia, so far on his way to solicit the protection of the emperor for his church. This he would, no doubt, readily obtain; for the Russians, like the ancient Romans, unite in a remarkable degree, the extremes of tolerance and superstition. There was, also, M. Hartung, a German, whose business in the metropolis was to teach the Guards to shoot. He had invented a very simple machine, by means of which an officer, standing behind a soldier about to fire, can direct his aim with unfailing accuracy. M. Hartung considered that a few lessons given in this manner would be worth half a lifetime of practice in the ordinary way; and the emperor seems also to have judged favourably of the plan, having bestowed a pension and an order upon the inventor. Hartung was a gunsmith, and is a simple, peaceable man, with no more thought of blood in his mind than an angler or a fowler!

We had, also, Count Lambsdorff, a son of the late amiable and excellent man, who was tutor to Nicolas, when grand duke; and, last, not least, a Russian merchant, with a most patriarchal beard, and a countenance strongly expressive of the mixture of acuteness and good nature which distinguishes his countrymen. With such variety in my companions, it may be supposed that the journey must have been a pleasant one; and so it was, notwithstanding that we foundered several times in the unfathomable ruts of the road.

On the second night, no efforts of the horses could get the vehicle out of one of those abysses into which it had sunk, and we were obliged to call in the assistance of the neighbouring peasants. The next night, we were all of us in like manner working hard for five hours in the middle of the highway; till, at length, a temporary road was constructed at the place of branches of trees, and the unwieldy carriage raised upon the new surface by main force. On the fourth night, a similar accident occurred, but of much shorter duration. The patience of the conducteur was by this time wholly exhausted. Snatching up a stick, he belaboured unmercifully the nearest postillion; he, in turn, horsewhipped with his whole strength and his whole mind the further one; and the latter laid it into his cattle with whip and spur, as if desirous of transferring the benefit of the whole flagellation to them. All this was accompanied by the most frightful cries, yells, and howlings; and, at length, by a mighty effort, the huge machine was torn out of its bed of mud, and rolled upon terra firma.

The scenery of Livonia does not differ in any remarkable degree from that of Courland; and the manners of the people, though these were originally distinct races, are pretty nearly the same. The Livonian peasants, however, are still more solitary than the Courlanders. They rarely live in villages, but continue to inhabit the rude and lonely huts of their ancestors. The diet of both is black bread and barley-gruel; the former made of rye, ground without any preparation, and the latter occasionally enriched with vegetables, or, in autumn, even with pork. It is then they are rich; it is then they kill their pigs (of which each farmer has in general two) for the winter; and it is then there is marrying, and giving in marriage, in Courland and Livonia.

But the honey-moon does not last long. Their pigs, their grain, their vegetables, all are devoured in the dreary winter which succeeds; and spring, the season of gladness to others, to them comes chilly and sternly on. The ground is yet covered with snow; the sod is a frozen mass; the womb of the earth is shut.

Scarcely able to live themselves, what becomes of their cattle? When the stock of hay is drawing to a close, the remainder is sparingly mixed with straw for the cows, while the horses subsist upon straw alone. The latter animals are small, but surprisingly hardy. After such lean diet, they are set to work the moment the ground thaws. It is true, they often fall down from exhaustion after an hour's labour; but, in this case, they are only turned into a neighbouring morass, where they contrive to pick up as many of the scarcely visible blades of vegetation, as suffice to set them on their legs again for an hour more.

Spring, however, has its compensations. At this season the heart softens like the bosom of the earth, and the blood runs free, like a stream disenchanted from the spells of winter. Love is the earliest flower of the spring, and it raises its head amidst cold, and poverty, and hunger: it is in autumn, when the pigs and peasants are fat, that Hymen lights his prosaic torch. But there is not much of

poetry it must be owned, at least in the locality
chosen by the Livonian Cupid, which is the stable
and cow-house of the lord of the land. It is the
duty of the peasants at this epoch, in addition to
their other allotted tasks, to clean these Augean
depôts; and they await impatiently a call which
promises both warmth and good cheer. When the
day arrives, they hasten, in joyous processions, to
the scene, singing and dancing as they go; and, in
the steaming warmth of the cow-house, the luxury
of an unstinted meal, and the exhiliration of the
national votki, the whiskey of Russia, they forget
the cold and hunger of winter, and give themselves
up to merriment and flirtation.

As the season advances, the love which was thus
planted in a hot-house, ripens in the open air; and,
by the autumn following, the harvest is ready.
The flowers of passion are then gathered in for
household use. It is true, they thus lose their
beauty and their flavour; but the epoch is, for all
that, a season of rejoicing; and here, as well as
every where else, men celebrate with shouts of
mirth, the moment when the glory of their fields
and hearts is laid low. The house of the bride is
surmounted by a huge plume of feathers, ribbons,
and rags, of every form and hue, and her door is
arched round with branches and flowers. At two
o'clock on Sunday morning, she hears a knock at
that door, and feels as if it had been struck upon
her heart. She does not answer—transmitted custom forbids!—and the comers are obliged to bribe

the family to disclose her retreat. These are the friends selected to conduct the ceremony, and who are under the obligation to defray every expense preliminary to the moment of union.

The hours are spent in drinking till it is time to go to church; when a relation of the bride gives the signal for starting by taking down the plume from the roof, and mounting with it on horseback. In this state he leads the procession, and the destined fair one follows, with her female friends, in a carriage borrowed for the occasion. The bride is usually dressed like a French lady; for her mistress would be very austere indeed, if, on so interesting an occasion, she refused the loan of almost any part of her wardrobe. The cavalcade visits the lord of the land, and other rich neighbours, to all of whom the virgin offers a pair of gloves, stockings, or garters, receiving in return a present of money. When passing the bridge of the town or village in which the church is situated, she throws a pair of garters among the crowd; and lucky is that individual who, in the general scramble which ensues, obtains possession of the prize. After the marriage ceremony is performed in the usual way, the procession returns in the same order, celebrating the event by shouting and firing pistols. The whole party then repair to the bridegroom's house; and both sexes sit down to a feast, from which they rarely think of rising till mid-day on Monday.

The new home of the bride, like her old one, consists in general of two apartments. One of them

is the place for drying the grain, which is spread
upon the stove, and on shelves near the roof, where
the air is hottest ; an operation which enables them
to keep the article, if necessary, for years. In this
apartment they sleep in the winter months ; the
married couple on mattresses upon the floor, and the
others on benches that are ranged along the walls.
Sometimes, in the more substantial houses, the
corner occupied by the master and mistress of the
family is separated from the rest of the room by
curtains; but in general this distinction is dispensed
with.

In the second apartment the grain is thrashed,
and this is the summer dormitory. Night is the
time chosen for thrashing the grain, and after the
exercise, all stretch themselves without ceremony
upon the floor, or on the benches. This strange
custom is *not* productive of immorality. The
peasant girls of Courland and Livonia are like those
of other countries ; and their popular ballads turn
still more than usual upon the beauty and value of
female honour. Some of their rude poems describe
the solicitations to which the heroine was subjected
from her lord, and the successful stratagems by
means of which she escaped.

Our young bride, up to the moment in which we
saw her fairly lodged in her conjugal home, had
always been reckoned, like many of her companions,
a pretty girl ; but a shade of care and anxiety now
descends upon her brow, and her beauty vanishes
trace by trace. The object of her existence appears

to be attained; the dreams that lightened her labours have vanished; her work augments, while its
compensations diminish; her mirror is forsaken as
a useless toy; her dress is neglected; and, already
old in heart, a few years suffice to make her old in
aspect.

The peasants of Courland, Livonia, and Esthonia,
are commonly said to be free, since they no longer
belong to the land or to the nobles; but, in reality,
they are only progressing towards a state of freedom,
for as yet they cannot choose their own professions,
but must remain cultivators till the population of
the provinces reaches a certain amount.

A very great mistake has been committed by most
writers on this subject, and one which precludes
the possibility of any accurate idea being formed, of
the nature and value of the experiment instituted
by Alexander, and now in progress. The peasants
have been confounded by these inquirers with the
nobles; and, it being assumed that the "inhabitants" already possessed a greater degree of liberty
than the other Russians, the step, it has been taken
for granted, towards a still farther extension of this
inestimable blessing, was easy and natural. Now
the fact is completely otherwise. During the short
period of the Swedish dominion in these countries,
the nobles became civilized; and, as a natural consequence, endeavoured to spread the advantages of
civilization among their barbarous vassals. Their
pride was interested, as well as their better feelings,
in the well-doing of their dependants; and the

E

comparative emancipation of the latter, by destroying
the mutual bonds between lord and serf, has been as
yet productive of any thing but good to either
party. That the good will come, and the measure
ultimately prove to have been a wise one, cannot be
doubted; but, in the meantime, the advocates of
freedom should not elude the question, or endeavour
to disguise the evils to which even a necessary
reform has given birth.

The present system is simply this. The estates
are parcelled out by their owners in small farms,
and valued, not by themselves, but by a commission,
in rubles and kopeks. The tenants take their farms
at the value established by the commission, which
they agree to pay, not in money, but in labour. At
stated times, a man on foot, or on horseback, as
may be arranged, is put at the disposal of the landlord; and the service, extending to a certain number of days in the year, is calculated at a fixed rate.
A field is also cultivated for his behoof; and the
whole amount of such services forms the rent of the
farm. Each farmer has in general three or four
male assistants residing on the spot, and about as
many females. The former, if married, are assigned
a field, which they cultivate for themselves; if
unmarried, the field is cultivated by the master-
farmer. In the case of any misunderstanding, the
farmer may complain at once to the governor of the
province, and his complaint is readily listened to.
He may also remove, on going through certain
legal formalities, from one farm to another.

This, so far as it goes, is liberty; but the people do not, as yet, comprehend the word. They seek to change their master, thinking that change is liberty. They neglect the fields which they do not now look upon as their own; and their landlord neglects the servants who in a few months may be his no longer. Too ignorant to become really independent, their existence is a continued series of famine and repletion. When the year is good, the farmer, instead of preserving his money for future exigencies, lays it out in horses and cows, which he is speedily obliged to sell. All these, however, are merely the evils of ignorance. Slavery, the great barrier against civilization has been overthrown; and I venture to predict, that, fifty years hence, the traveller in the Baltic provinces of Russia will find a free and flourishing peasantry.

The nobles of these provinces are almost all of German descent, and their lands are the ancient fiefs of the Brothers of the Sword. This confraternity, although often confounded with that of the Teutonic Knights, was, in reality, completely distinct, and was formed at the commencement of the thirteenth century, for the express purpose of conquering Livonia to Christianity. In 1238, they adopted the rules of the Teutonic order, and united themselves to that body, but without giving up their own identity. Their grand master became sovereign, while the Teutonic grand master reigned in Prussia. It was in 1550 that an invasion of the Russians overthrew this military empire; when the grand master sunk into Duke of Courland, and the rest of his dominions became the property of Sweden and Poland.

At the present day, Livonia is peopled half by Letts and half by Esthonians, and the latter are said to retain much of their hostility to their German lords. The Cours are more reconciled; while the Letts are as yet hardly emerged from the indifference of apathy.

It was at Dorpat that we found the Esthonian population of Livonia commence. This town is said to have been founded by Iaroslaf I., at the beginning of the eleventh century, the province having then made part of the Russian dominions. No trace, however, of such respectable antiquity is now visible. The place has been so often burnt down that at this moment it is quite new, and is indeed a very handsome little town. Its university was founded in 1632 by Gustavus Adolphus; but, in the time of Olearius was so little known as to boast only about a score of students, half Swedes and half Fins. It was re-established by the emperor Paul, and is at present a school of great respectability.

On leaving Dorpat, I saw a very unfavourable specimen of the Esthonian peasantry. The sample consisted of about a dozen young women, so like each other that, in a smaller number, they must have been taken for sisters. All had the same lank, uncombed yellow hair hanging over their shoulders, the same light, meaningless eyes, and the same fishy complexion; and all were arrayed in a garb so ingeniously contrived to conceal the shape, that I was for some time in doubt as to their sex.

A village next attracted my attention, on the right-hand side of the road—if it be lawful to call such a thing a village. It consisted of thirty or forty of the most wretched huts that can be conceived, open, one would think, in all quarters, to wind and weather, and yet each possessing, no doubt, some central hole where the family might burrow in warmth and filth. These habitations were set down without the smallest regard to a general plan; and not even the earliest rudiments of a street could be detected. It seemed as if the people, though compelled to live in society, had resolved to preserve each his own solitary and distinctive character inherited from his ancestors; and thus the place gave one the idea,—if such a thing can be conceived,—of a village of hermits.

This was, in some degree, the general character of the villages between Dorpat and Narva; but with one very remarkable exception, occurring on the banks of the lake Peipus. This immense sheet of water, seventy-five miles long, and thirty-eight broad, lay in utter lifelessness between its level banks, the further side lost in the hazy distance. Three or four small oar-boats specked its surface, manned, no doubt, though we could not see them, by some sleepy fishermen; but no sails floated along its bosom, not a single symptom appeared of the activity either of business or pleasure. Built upon the brink of this tranquil sea, stood the village in question. The houses, like those of all the Russian villages which we were destined to see, were formed of the trunks of pines stripped of the bark, and their ends, at the corners of the building, locked into each other with the nicest precision. The gables were towards the road, connected together by large gates, or walls of the same material; and the over-arching part of the roof was neatly ornamented with such plain sculpture as the axe can execute. All was uniform, all clean, and the general effect was not only pleasing but handsome. At this place we did not see a single human being, even at the windows. The answer my fellow-travellers made to my inquiries was unintelligible at the time, and will perhaps surprise some of my readers: "It is, no doubt, *a colony of Russians*—a crown village."

The environs of Narva are extremely picturesque; and, as we passed through the citadel, the majestic ruins of the old and new fortress touched the scene with an effect not unallied to sublimity. I was desirous, however, of expending the little time I had in a visit to the celebrated falls of the Narova; and we no sooner arrived at the station, than after negociating with the conducteur of the diligence, I took post horses, and set off at full gallop for the spot, in the only vehicle that could be obtained at the moment—an open cart.

I remember having been disappointed by the great fall of Schaffhausen, and I was so in like manner by that of the Narova. It did not, in fact, correspond with my idea of a fall at all. I saw only a mass of black and boiling waters, extending a considerable distance up and down the river, here and there broken into white foam, and deserving the name of a torrent rather than that of a cataract. But when I had placed myself upon the middle of a wooden bridge, which spans the flood in the most *impossible* situation imaginable, the spectacle presented itself in a new aspect, and I was able to account for the reputation enjoyed by the " Fall."

Immediately opposite the spectator, as he looks up the river, the torrent breaks upon a ledge of rocks, and performs a furious and headlong descent of a few feet. This is not sufficient to constitute a great fall in itself ; but it is the *point d'appui* of the whole scene. Here centre the rush and the roar of the far-extending volume of water before you ; and the mind unconsciously invests with the attributes of power, magnitude, and passion, which in reality belong to the river, that single spot more imme-diately and prominently presented to its percep-tions.

Even making allowance, however, for such invo-luntary illusions, I cannot conceive how Mr. Rae Wilson could have supposed the fall to be a thousand feet broad, and four hundred and seventy-three feet high ! At the spot I allude to, where alone there is any thing at all resembling a fall, the river is just a hundred paces broad, and the descent of the water over the rocks is certainly within the computation of Herbinius—twelve feet. The four hundred and seventy-three feet mentioned by Mr. Wilson, if not a mistake altogether, must be the descent of the river in a course of at least half a mile. The account given by the old traveller Olearius, possesses a quality of imagination of quite a different kind, and its truth as well as beauty will strike every one who visits the Narova.

"About half a league above this town," says he, "there is a fall of water, which makes a dreadful noise, and is so violent, that breaking upon the rocks it is reduced, as it were, to powder, which filling the air, affords a strange sight, by reason that the sun shining upon it, makes a kind of rainbow no less pleasant than that framed in the clouds."

After leaving Narva (once a Hanseatic town!) we crossed the river Laga on a flying bridge. It was now dark, and the embarkation took place by torch-light. The scene was worth the study either of a poet or painter; and the tumbling, rushing, and roaring of the black waters of the river added enough of the idea of danger to keep our feelings on the stretch. The operation was superintended by soldiers in uniform, whose figures contrasted finely with those of the shaggy, sheepskinned peasants who conducted the moving bridge. When coach, horses, and passengers were at length fairly on board, and we found ourselves gliding out into the torrent, whose mystic forms were distorted by the lights that danced brokenly on the surges, I would not for a few minutes have exchanged feelings with any hero of romance who ever launched upon the sea of adventure, to tumble on for a time in danger, darkness, and mystery—and then land safe and sound upon terra firma!

From this place to St. Petersburg, the scenery may be said to have been entirely without relief. As soon as there was light enough, a dreary flat presented itself, with here and there a jungle or morass, and a few huts on the brink of the cheerless horizon. As we advanced, this expanse became almost entirely covered with snow; and groups of peasants, men and women, engaged in clearing it, amounting in all I should think to some thousands, lined the road. Occasionally the passengers were obliged to descend and wade through the snow themselves. Every thing gave us to understand that we had entered the government of St. Petersburg, where the climate is severer than in any other civilized country in the world; and where at this moment the highway, covered with the snows of winter, and broken up by the thaws of spring, enjoyed the advantages of neither season.

It was not till after we had crossed the flying-bridge that we had fairly entered Russia. Till then we had traversed the governor-generalships of Courland and Livonia, and a portion of that of Esthonia, of which the capitals are Mittau, Riga, and Revel. The inhabitants of those provinces in the middle ages were various struggling tribes, afterwards conquered successively by Russians, Poles, Danes, Swedes, and Germans. Under so many masters, the people of course sunk into the lowest state of servage; and, indeed, it was not till the late reign that any general attempt was made to elevate them to their proper rank in the creation.

While the peasants remain in a state of ignorance, the proprietors will, as a matter of course, remain poor. This is, in a great measure, the condition of both at present, but a rapid change for the better is in progress. The system of territorial loan-banks, which prevails in all the three provinces, is one great means of keeping up the resources of the landholders. These banks lend to the proprietor upon mortgage, in such a manner, that if the interest is regularly paid the principal can never be demanded. If the interest is not paid, the bank takes the estate into its own hands, and continues to manage it till the deficiency is made up; and the land then returns to its owner. In Courland there is this difference, that a small sinking fund upon the principal is required every year. In Courland, also, the interest is five per cent, while in Livonia and Esthonia it has been reduced from that rate to four.

On quitting Esthonia the change in the appearance of the population is very perceptible, and not very pleasing. Some of the women of that province, in spite of their lank yellow hair, are tolerably good looking; while here, the fair sex as yet are clad with just as little regard to the picturesque; and are besides—we speak it under correction—stumpy and ugly.

It was the middle of the night before we reached St. Petersburg. The streets were deserted, except by the watchmen, who stood here and there at

Drawn by A. G. Vickers.

Engraved by H. Jorden.

The Troitskoi Church on the Fontanka Canal.

St. Petersburg.

London. Published Octr 1 1852, for the Proprietors, by Longman & Co Paternoster Row; Hinrich & Co Leipzig; Asher, Berlin.

regular distances, each armed with a pole-axe. Every thing was as silent as the grave; and at an hour when London is traversed by hurrying crowds, and the houses shaken by the roll of carriages, I found the great northern metropolis buried in profound slumber. My first impression was amazement at the gigantic scale on which the city appeared to be laid out, and the stupendous forms of the objects around me; but when we rolled past the magnificent bridge over the Fontanka. I could hardly contain my impatience till the morning. With the accurate and beautiful representation of this bridge, and the church of the Trinity in the neighbourhood, which is annexed, I bespeak the interest of the reader for the notices I am about to lay before him of the various parts of St. Petersburg.

We at length reached the Diligence Hotel, an advertisement of which, boasting, among other advantages, of its reasonable terms, I had seen in every inn on the road, and here I took up my abode for the remainder of the night. Here too I had reason to be surprised at the great scale on which things are conducted in St. Petersburg: the price of a bed-room, destitute of almost every comfort and convenience, was five rubles !

CHAPTER IV.

Origin of St. Petersburg—first appearance of Peter the Great
on the banks of the Neva—idea of the localities—construction of the fortress—manner of building—progress of the
works— the log-hut palace—influx of population—mysterious marriage of the Tsar—marriage of the dwarfs—
funeral of the dwarf-husband—first book printed at St.
Petersburg—compulsory increase of the city—discontent
of the people—triumph and death of the Tsar.

THE site of Petersburg may be said to have
belonged from time immemorial to the Russians.
The republic of Novgorod may be looked upon as a
rebel power springing up in times of tumult and
disaster; and when Ivan III. in the fifteenth
century, brought under his sway the whole of its
dependencies, he only gathered together the divided
provinces of Russia.

The Neva was then, as it had been for several
centuries before, the grand highway of the external
commerce of Novgorod ; and Ingria on the left

bank, and Carelia on the right, had been more than once a debatable land of bloodshed between the forces of the republic and those of the invading Swedes. The latter at length, after experiencing various fortunes, in the course of which they were sometimes masters of the province, and were sometimes expelled, taking advantage of the distracted state of the country in the beginning of the seventeenth century, obtained firm possession of Ingria and Carelia, which eventually were surrendered to them in 1617 by the treaty of Stolbof.

The Swedes made good use of their conquest. They built a town called Nyen, at the confluence of the Okhta with the Neva (nearly opposite the Smolnoi monastery of to-day) which became, although only for a short time, a famous mart of commerce. Peter the Great, however, was not likely to allow the maritime frontiers of his kingdom to remain long in the hands of a foreign power. He directed his utmost resources to the re-conquest of the Neva; and in the month of April, 1703, we find him, in the rank of a captain of grenadiers, marching under the orders of his own general, along those wild and dreary banks where a stupendous city was one day to be called into being by the enchantments of his genius.

The fortress of Nyen soon fell, and a Swedish fleet which, unconscious of the circumstance, appeared at the mouth of the river, was destroyed by a party in boats headed by the Tsar in person. Peter was thus master of the Neva, the grand avenue of com-

merce to the centre of his dominions; and the
question naturally became, how to secure the con-
quests he had gained.

The whole country around was a forest or a
marsh. The darkness of these primeval woods was
only relieved here and there by a gleam of water,
which showed that they were nearly impassable by
the foot of man. A few huts on the edge of the
river were tenanted by savage natives, who lived
upon the fish of the Neva, and the rewards they
sometimes received for piloting the Swedish barks
up the stream. It was here the Tsar determined to
found a mighty and magnificent city.

Before the Neva falls into the Gulf of Finland, it
sends off two branches to the right, and the three
streams form the grand outline of its delta.
Exactly midway between these two branches, there
was a very small island, separated from the right bank
only by a narrow channel. The main body of the
river, therefore, was in its front, the small channel
behind, and behind that an immense morass; while
on either side an arm of the Neva embraced the
morass, of which they formed an island. It was
this spot which Peter chose for his citadel; and here
he set to work with an earnestness of enthusiasm, a
" regia animositas," which has few parallels in
history.

It was necessary to elevate the surface of the
little island by means of earth transferred from other
places—to cut timber—to transport stones—even
before the actual task of constructing the fortress

commenced; and the number of labourers required was, therefore, immense. These consisted not only of the troops—of the Swedish prisoners—of the neighbouring Ingrians and Carelians—even of the people of Olonetz and Novgorod; but also of vast numbers of labourers from the interior governments of the empire—of Cossacks, Tatars, Kalmuks, brought hither from their distant solitudes to build a city between the Baltic and the White Sea. Forty thousand men were thus employed at one time; races, tongues, and creeds were intermixed; and the young women of the Neva, the mothers of the future capital, received husbands from the banks of the Don and the Volga.

To provide instruments of labour for such a multitude would have swallowed up a revenue much greater than Peter's. Besides, that was their own affair. The Tsar merely commanded them to do such a thing—he did not interfere with the mode in which they were to set about it. They had neither pickaxes, nor hatchets, nor shovels, nor carts; but they had their fingers to dig, their hands wherewith to carry, and, if more was necessary, they could turn their caftans into sacks. In this manner the work progressed with a rapidity which seems astonishing. In a few weeks the face of nature was changed, and instead of two fishing-huts in ruins, the only original habitations on the island, their arose the walls of a formidable fortress. It is needless to say, that in the meantime the workmen slept upon the damp ground, and in the open air; and that it was very often a matter of impossibility in such a wilderness as this, to supply forty thousand Elijahs with their daily meal. The building of St. Petersburg it is calculated, cost the lives of upwards of three hundred thousand men.

In four months the fortress was completed, and named in honour of the apostle. It contained a wooden church dedicated to the apostles Peter and Paul, on the three spires of which a ship's flag was hoisted on Sundays and festivals. The roofs of the houses were covered, in the Finnish fashion, with turf or birch bark. To the south of the church, where the commandant's house is now placed, there was a corps de garde, with two ornaments in front curiously characteristic of the time and the country. These were the wooden figure of a horse with its back forming an edge as sharp as could be produced, and a post surrounded by a narrow circle of stakes, the upper ends cut to a fine point. On the horse convicted culprits were seated astride; on the post they were placed standing.

The imperial palace was not in the fortress but close by. It was a common log-house, fifty-six feet long and twenty-one broad, and contained two apartments, one on each side of the door, and a little bedroom the breadth of the passage to fill up. This edifice was painted outside to resemble brick; and the interior, instead of tapestry, was hung with coarse canvass painted white. The ceiling, with its large rude joints, was covered in like manner; and the ridge of the roof was adorned with a mortar in the centre, and at each end with a bomb in sculptured wood. M. Bachoutsky calls the bed-room a kitchen; but its only entrance is from one of the principal apartments, and besides it is covered, roof and walls, with white canvass like the others. The kitchin doubtless was altogether apart from the cottage, according to a custom very general in the Russian houses. Menchikoff, the favourite, lived immediately opposite the Tsar, but in so spacious a house that his master was fain to borrow it sometimes on the occasion of grand audiences. These, with the tents and huts which the workmen now began to construct in preparation for the approaching winter, formed the city of St. Petersburg one hundred and thirty-two years ago.

In the following two years, many private houses were built near the imperial abode, all of wood, all of one story, without court, and without any general plan; and on the opposite, or left bank of the Neva, a range of humble cottages began to line the river. The population increased daily. The Tatars and Kalmuks, and other workmen from distant parts of the empire, were contented to sit down, after their labours at the fortress were over, and to find on the Gulf of Finland an abiding place and a continuing city. Fins, Esthonians, Livonians, all fled from the tumult of war, and took refuge under the wings of the imperial eagle. Even the Swedes themselves who had been driven from their homes, came to beg for refuge in St. Petersburg. Tradesmen, labourers, sailors, flocked hither in thousands with their wives

and families, in search of a subsistence; and, as a
natural consequence of this sudden increase of inhabitants, the new city became the resort of pedlars
and merchants of every description. All were
welcomed with open arms. Land and timber were
given away in profusion. The captain of the first
foreign ship—a Dutchman—received a present of
five hundred ducats, and each of the crew three
hundred dollars. Thus the great work went on,
with a rapidity which, if all these accompanying
circumstances were unknown, would be reckoned
marvellous, if not incredible.

The intelligent reader will here observe, without
any suggestion of mine, the origin of that religious
toleration which at the present day has set down in
this city no fewer than seven different temples of
seven different creeds, in a single street. When the
priests of the other churches have occasion to mention the Greek faith, they call it merely what it
really is, the "dominant" or prevailing "religion of
the country."

In 1707 the streets of St. Petersburg already
began to take some form, for the Tsar was discon-
tented with their irregularity; and some ship-building
yards were established on the site of those of the
present Admiralty. Towards the winter of that
year Peter again visited the city, and proceded as
usual to his cabin-palace near the fortress. At
nightfall he ordered his sledge, and stepping into it
with a lady, desired Bruce, the commandant, to get
up behind. They dashed across the river, which

was frozen over, turned to the right, in the direction which leads to the sea, and plunging through the woods which covered their savage tract, arrived at a little wooden church near the embouchure of the Fontanka. The little church was almost buried in snow, but they contrived to effect an entrance; and Bruce having led in a priest, and lighted a few feet around them by means of a solitary lamp, Peter the Great was there and then married to the Empress Catharine the First. What church this was it is impossible now to say, and even the precise date of these extraordinary nuptials is unknown to history!

It is not my hint to speak of the various perils undergone by the infant city. It surmounted them all; and in the seventh year of its existence was the scene of a ceremony very different from the above. Peter liked all ceremonies of which he himself was not the ostensible hero. If his destiny had connected him with the stage, he would have been a prompter and not an actor. Nay, he carried this kind of modesty so far that it actually amounted to mauvaise honte, and caused him to blush like a girl. This was particularly observed at the public and brilliant reception of the Persian ambassador in 1723, three years after he had received the richly merited titles of Peter the Great, Father of his Country, and Emperor of all the Russias.

On the present occasion, however, the nuptials of his niece the Tsarevna Anna Ivanovna with the Duke of Courland, presented the first public spectacle on an extended scale which the citizens of Petersburg

had seen. The imperial family, the foreign ministers, and the principal grandees of Russia, were
present ; and these had the satisfaction of seeing the
greatest man of his age enact the part of master of
the ceremonies at a girl's wedding. Peter performed
his duty with the same zealous enthusiasm which
distinguished the founder of Petersburg, and the
conqueror of Pultava. He paraded the streets in
his quality of first marshal of the day, with music
playing before him ; and during the banquet went
round the table, decorated with an immense shoul-
der-knot of lace and ribbons, serving the guests, and
forcing them to do justice to the good things he set
before them. It is not upon record that he actually
pocketed the keys of the house ; but we know
that it was expressly forbidden to any one to retire
without leave of the Tsar ; which leave was not
granted till two o'clock in the morning.

The entertainment which followed, given by
Menchikoff, the favourite of the Tsar, is well known,
at which two dwarfs were served up to the company in two gigantic pies. The Russian grandees
have always been fond of dwarfs, and are so, in
some instances, at the present day; and Peter, more
especially, who was a man of splendid genius, but
not a miracle, delighted in these unfortunate acci-
dents of nature.* The famous Marriage of the
Dwarfs, which took place also on the occasion of the

---

* The dwarfs still to be seen in the houses of the Russian nobility,—and
I do not think they amount to more than half a dozen for the whole
empire,—are no longer buffoons but domestic servants.

above nuptials, is the most stupendous thing in little which the world ever beheld.

Seventy-two dwarfs, of both sexes, were assembled at Petersburg to assist at the marriage. The little marshal of the day headed the cortege, and then, hand in hand, came the little bride and bridegroom. Immediately after their littlenesses came Peter the Great and his suite; and then, two and two, the rest of the dwarfs and dwarfesses—followed, as may well be supposed, by every living soul in St. Petersburg. The marriage ceremony took place in the church of Saint Peter and Saint Paul, in the fortress, and all then repaired to the hotel of Menchikoff, where they partook of a splendid repast.

One feels sorry to pursue the history of this singular union. Nine or ten months after, the poor bride died an agonizing death in bringing forth a dead child; and the circumstance occasioned an edict against the marriage of dwarfs. The husband survived her a dozen years, but his life was embittered by his own bad conduct, and the consequent loss of the favour of the Tsar. His funeral, however, was conducted with all the grotesque magnificence of his bridal. The cortege assembled in that part of the Winter Palace which is near the Hermitage; and, headed by six infant choristers, and the smallest priest that could be found in the city, took the way to the Nevski Prospekt. The dead body was carried in a hearse drawn by six dwarf ponies, guarding which on each side was a long line of gigantic soldiers, clothed in black mantles, and each holding a lighted torch in his hand. The dwarfs then came, marching two and two, the males first, and the females after; but, on reaching the Nevski Prospekt, they were put into immense chariots, drawn by great horses. Here the emperor, who had so far accompanied the procession, returned to his palace; and the little mourners were driven on to Iamskaïa, where they deposited their comrade in the earth, according to the forms of the Greek church.

About this epoch of the city the first post-house was built, and then the first tavern (frequented by Peter himself), and last, not least, the first printing establishment. For thirteen years before, the Russian books had all been printed at Amsterdam, and previous to that period, at Moscow. The following is the title of the first book produced by the press of St. Petersburg, " The Book of Mars; or exploits of the Russian warriors of his Tsarian Majesty, at the taking of superb fortifications, and on different fields of battle, exploits executed against the troops of his Swedish Majesty."

Although the city continued to increase with a rapidity approaching the marvellous, considering the nature of the ground, it failed to keep pace with the wishes of the Tsar. In 1714, he published an oukaz, compelling three hundred and fifty noble families to remove from Moscow and other places, and build themselves houses in St. Petersburg, on the locations assigned to them. The same extraor-

dinary measure was taken with regard to the merchants and artizans, each of which classes was
ordered forthwith to build three hundred houses.
Peter also compelled his barbarian subjects to adopt
the rules of politeness ; and, by introducing assem-
blies and soirées, and teaching his bears to dance,
he rescued from a state of savage degradation, and
elevated to her natural sphere in society, that
civilizer of man—Woman.

The Russians, however, were not at that time
qualified to comprehend and appreciate the designs
of a man of genius ; and it required all the energy
of Peter to sweep aside the obstacles that were perpetually thrown in his way. At one time, a spirit
of prophecy seized the opponents of civilization,
and a "Wo!—wo!" was preached to the citizens,
calling upon them to prepare for speedy destruction.
On another occasion, the image of the Virgin in the
church of the Trinity was made to shed tears.
Murmurs were heard, and tumultuous meetings seen
on all sides ; but the Tsar, turning neither to the
right nor to the left, carried through his designs
with the strong hand. If ever absolute sovereignty
was beneficial to a people, it was in this instance.
Peter effected more in a single life-time than society
left to itself could have achieved in many genera-
tions.

That valuable life was not much longer spared to
Russia and mankind. Twenty-two years after the
foundation of St. Petersburg, Peter the Great terminated his busy, useful, and glorious career

To pursue further the advance of the city would far exceed the limits of my little book. The building of palaces, besides, and the erection of monuments in the usual way are, comparatively speaking, vulgar and uninteresting affairs. Perhaps, however, the reader will not grudge the few pages which I have devoted to the foregoing sketch. Such, at all events, could not fail to have been my reflections, or my inquiries, with my foot upon the threshold of St. Petersburg.

CHAPTER V.

First idea of the aspect of St. Petersburg—want of individuality in its physical character—grandeur of the scale on which it is built—construction of the streets—curious wooden pavement—houses and mode of building—general character of the city—first idea of the population—vehicles and drivers—artizans and labourers—dislike to machinery —extraordinary ladder and scaffold—perilous situations of the workmen—mujik from the interior—female peasants —grand distinctive characteristic of the population.

St. Petersburg has been frequently called "the most magnificent city in Europe," but the expression appears to me to be wholly destitute of meaning. Venice is a magnificent city, so is Paris, so is St. Petersburg; but there are no points of *comparison* among them. St. Petersburg is a city of new houses, newly painted. The designs of some of them may be old, but the copies are evidently new. They imitate the classic models; but they often imitate them badly, and there is always something to remind one that they are not the genuine classic. They are like the images which the

G

Italian boys carry about the thoroughfares of London
—Venuses de Medici and Belvidere Apollos, in
stucco.

But the streets are wide, and the walls painted
white or light yellow; and from one street opens
another, and another, and another—all wide, and
white, and light yellow.   And then, here and there,
there are columned façades, and churches, and
domes, and tapering spires—all white too, that are
not gilded, or painted a sparkling green.   And
canals sweep away to the right and left almost at
every turning, not straight and Dutch-like, but
bending gracefully, and losing themselves among
the houses.   And there is one vast and glorious
river, as wide as the Thames at London, and a
hundred times more beautiful, which rolls through
the whole; and, beyond it, from which ever side
you look, you see a kindred mass of houses and
palaces, white and yellow, and columned façades,
and churches, and domes, and spires, gilded and
green.

The left bank of this river is a wall of granite,
with a parapet and trottoir of the same material,
extending for several miles; and this forms one of
the most magnificent promenades in Europe.   The
houses on either side look like palaces, for all are
white, and many have columns; and there are also
absolute *de facto* palaces; for instance, the Admiralty, the Winter Palace, and the Marble Palace, on
one side, and the Academy of Arts, on the other.
The water in the middle is stirring with boats,

leaping and sweeping through the stream, with lofty, old-fashioned sterns, painted and gilded within and without.

Among the streets, there is one averaging the width of Oxford Street in London, sometimes less, sometimes a little more. It is lined with trees, and shops with painted shutters, and churches of half a dozen different creeds. Its shops, indeed, are not so splendid as ours, nor are their windows larger than those of private houses; but the walls are white and clean, sometimes columned, sometimes pillastered, sometimes basso-relievoed: in fact, if you can imagine such a thing as a street of *gin-palaces* just after the painting season—and that is a bold word—you may form an idea scarcely exaggerated of the Nevski Prospekt.

But no analogy taken from London can convey an idea of the—grandeur, I may venture to say, presented by the vistas opening from the main street. Here there are no lanes, no alleys, no *impasses*, no nestling-places constructed of filth and rubbish for the poor. These lateral streets are all parts of the main street, only diverging at right angles. The houses are the same in form and colour; they appear to be inhabited by the same classes of society; and the view is terminated, ever and anon by domes and spires. The whole, in short, is one splendid picture, various in its forms, but consistent in its character.

Such were my first impressions—thus thrown down at random, without waiting to look for words, and hardly caring about ideas,—the first sudden

impressions flashed upon my mind by the physical
aspect of St. Petersburg.

I have said in a former volume of this work,
that I have the custom,—like other idlers, I
suppose,—of wandering about during the first day
of my visit to a foreign city, without apparent
aim or purpose; without knowing, or desiring to
know, the geography of the place; and without
asking a single question.   Now this is precisely the
sort of view which should be taken of the new city
of the Tsars, by one who prefers the poetry of life
to its dull and hackneyed prose.   St. Petersburg is
a picture rather than a reality—grand, beautiful,
and noble, at a little distance, but nothing more
than a surface of paint and varnish when you look
closer.   Or, rather, to amend the comparison, it is
like the scene of a theatre, which you must not by
any means look behind, if you would not destroy the
illusion.

It will be said, that such is the case with all
cities, with all objects that derive their existence
from the puny sons of men: but this is one of those
misnamed truisms which are considered worthy of
all acceptation for no other reason than that they
come from the tongue, or through a neighbouring
organ, with the twang of religion or morality.

London does not lose but gain by inspection;
although on inspection it is found to be an enormous
heap of dirty, paltry, miserable brick houses,
which, but for the constant repairs of the inhabitants, would in a few years become a mass of such

pitiful ruins as the owls themselves would disdain
to inhabit. Those narrow, winding, dingy streets—
those endless lines of brick boxes, without taste,
without beauty, without dignity, without anything
that belongs to architecture, inspire us with growing
wonder and admiration. The genius, the industry,
the commerce, of a whole continent seem concen-
trated in this single spot ; and the effect is uninter-
rupted by any of the lighter arts that serve as the
mere ornaments and amusements of life. An earnestness of purpose is the predominating character
of the scene—a force of determination which seizes,
and fixes, and grapples with a single specific object,
to the exclusion of every other. The pursuit of
wealth acquires a character of sublimity as we gaze ;
and Mammon rises in majesty from the very deformity of the stupendous temple of commonplace
in which he is worshipped.

Venice does not lose but gain by inspection ;
although on inspection it is found to be but the
outlines of a great city, filled up with meanness, and
dirt, and famine. We enter her ruined palaces with
a catching of the breath, and a trembling of the
heart; and when we see her inhabitants crouching
in rags and hunger in their marble halls, we do but
breathe the harder, and tremble the more. The
effect is *increased* by the contrast; for Venice is a
tale of the past, a city of the dead. The Rialto is
still crowded with the shapes of history and romance ; the Giant's Steps still echo to the ducal
tread; and, mingling with the slaves and wantons

who meet on the Sunday evenings to laugh at the
rattle of their chains in the Piazza di San Marco,
we see gliding, scornful and sad, the merchant-kings
of the Adriatic.

St. Petersburg, on the other hand, has no moral
character to give dignity to common-place, or haunt
tombs and ruins like a spirit. It is a city of imita-
tation, constructed, in our own day, on what were
thought to be the best models; and hence the
severity with which its public buildings have been
criticised by all travellers, except those who dote
upon gilding and green paint, and are enthusiasts in
plaster and white-wash. As a *picture* of a city,
notwithstanding, superficially viewed—an *idea* of a
great congregating place of the human kind, without
reference to national character, or history, or individuality of any kind—St. Petersburg, in my opinion,
is absolutely unrivalled.

It would be difficult, even for the talented artist
whose productions grace these sketches, to convey
an adequate idea of the scale on which this city is
laid out; and yet, without doing so we do nothing.
This is the grand distinctive feature of the place.
Economy of room was the principal necessity in the
construction of the other great European cities; for,
above all things, they were to be protected from the
enemy by stone walls. But, before St. Petersburg
was built, a change had taken place in the art and
customs of war, and permanent armies had become
in some measure a substitute for permanent fortifications. Another cause of prodigality was the little

Drawn by A. G. Vickers.

Engraved by F. Radclyffe.

The Admiralty Square,
St Petersburg.

London, Published Oct.r 1, 1835, for the Proprietor, by Longman. & C.o Paternoster Row. Rittner & C.o Paris, & Asher Berlin.

value of the land; but, above all these, should be mentioned, the far-seeing, and far-thinking ambition of the builders. Conquest was the ruling passion of the Tsars from the beginning; and, in founding a new capital, they appear to have destined it to be the capital of half the world.

It is needless to exaggerate the magnitude of the city; as, for instance, some writers have done, by stating that the Nevski Prospekt is half as wide again as Oxford Street in London. Every thing is here on a gigantic scale. The quays, to which vessels requiring nine feet of water cannot ascend, except when the river is unusually high, might serve for all the navies of Europe. The public offices, or at least many of them, would hardly be too small, even if the hundred millions were added to the population of the country, which its soil is supposed to be capable of supporting.

Perhaps it may be as well to introduce here, for the sake of illustration, although a little prematurely as regards the description, a view of the grand square of the Admiralty. This is an immense oblong space in the very heart of the city. The spectator stands near the manège, the building which projects at the left-hand corner. Beyond this is the Admiralty, with its gilded spire, which is visible from almost all parts of the metropolis. Farther on is the Winter Palace, distinguished by a flag, in front of which, near the bottom of the vista, is the column raised to the memory of Alexander. Opposite this, on the right hand, is the palace of the

Etat Major, and returning towards the foreground, the War Office. The group in front are employed in dragging stones for the new Isaak's church, which stands in the left hand corner, although the view is not wide enough to admit it. This is to be the richest and most splendid building in the world; but it has been so long in progress, and is now so little advanced, that a notice of it must fall to the lot of some future traveller. Saint Isaak, I believe, is not particularly connected with Russia, except by his day falling upon the birth-day of Peter the Great.

Such is the scale on which St. Petersburg is built; for although this may be considered the heart of the city, the other members correspond. The very vastness of the vacant spaces, however, it should be observed, seems to make the houses on either side look less lofty; while on the other hand, no doubt the real want of loftiness in the houses exaggerates the breadth of the area between. But on the present occasion, any thing like fancy in the latter respect would have been quite supererogatory. The streets were hardly passable. Here and there a pond or a morass gave pause to the pedestrian; while the droski driver was only indebted to his daily renewed experience of the daily-changing aspect of the ground, for the comparative confidence and safety with which he pursued his way. The streets, in fact, were in the same predicament as the roads by which I had reached them; they had thawed from their winter consistence, and their stones, torn up, and dismantled by the severities of the frost, had not yet been put into summer quarters.

The greater part of the streets are what may be termed pebble-roads, a name which describes exactly what they are. At this moment, in the whole city, there are upwards of seven hundred and seventy-two thousand square sagenes* of these roads, while of stone pavement there are only nine thousand four hundred and fifty, and of wood six thousand four hundred.

The wooden pavement, I believe, is peculiar to St. Petersburg, and merits a description. It consists of small hexagons sawed from a piece of resinous wood, and laid into a bed formed of crushed stones and sand. These are fastened laterally into each other with wooden pegs, and when the whole forms a plain surface, the interstices are filled with fine sand, and then boiling pitch is poured over all. This pitch from the porous nature of the wood is speedily absorbed, and on a quantity of sand being strewed above it, the operation is complete, and a pavement constructed which is found to be extremely durable, and which seems to me to suffer much less injury from the frost than the stone causeway. The honour of the invention is due to M. Gourief; and I have no doubt he will ultimately see it adopted in most of the great towns towards the north. It is the custom of the peasants to cut down the trees at some distance from the root, and thus a great deal of

---

* A sagene is seven feet.

wood will be turned to a useful purpose which would otherwise only encumber the ground. Every peasant, besides, by means of his axe alone, is able to construct such a pavement, and in Russia hands are both plenty and cheap.

The construction of the houses, although I have described them as mere outsides, in regard to architectural beauty, is in general sufficiently solid. In the principal streets the outer wall of the ground floor—or rather the sunk floor, as the greater part of it is under-ground—is either granite or poudorsk (a stone of equal value found near Ijora), and the roof of this compartment of the house is usually vaulted. The other walls are of brick and deals, occasionally strengthened with iron bars. The flooring is of wood, and frequently a layer of brick and mortar is placed above it, and a second wooden floor laid over all. In some cases even a third floor, it is said, is added in the same way. The roof is always of sheet iron.

When the houses are built, they are left to dry for a year or more, according to their situation, before they are painted or stuccoed. After all they are cold and damp, from the circumstance of lath-work being unknown. If this was introduced as a lining to the outer walls, as well as for partitions, I have no doubt that the houses would be dryer and warmer, and inhabitable in half the time.

The general character of the place is not at all oriental, like that of the other Russian cities. There are a few buildings, indeed, that put you in

mind of the east—one hardly knows why, for in
reality there is nothing like them in Asia—but as a
whole, St. Petersburg is a jumble of classical forms,
often badly imitated and badly arranged. The
most striking of the exceptions are, perhaps, the
church of St. Nicolas, and the Smolnoi Monastery.
These buildings are two specimens of the ecclesiastical architecture of Russia; and the stranger, surrounded as he is by the orders of Greece and
Italy, cannot look upon their numerous onion-
shaped cupolas fantastically painted and gilded,
without feeling that he is in a country where, in
former times at least, some peculiar standard of
taste existed.

The strange thing is, that it is only in the roofs of
such buildings in Russia that their peculiarity exists.
Their façades are usually clustered with columns and
ornaments, taken from all sorts of classical models;
although, no doubt, the architect, by way of indem-
nifying his patriotic feelings, indulges here and there
in a little caricature or travestie. The churches
within the city, and the log-huts without—those are
Russian, those are national; and they have nothing
to do with St. Petersburg.

I am now lightly touching upon the general
character of the place,—laying the dim and indistinct
ground-work of my piece, before attempting to bring
out the individual features. It is impossible to do
this without noticing the living figures that give a
human interest to the scene.

The streets are never crowded, or else the spaces

are too large to appear so.   Even on the occasion of
a parade before the Winter Palace, when the troops
are inspected by the Emperor in person, they and
the spectators seem like a handful; the former on
the street, and the latter on the planted boulevard at
the side of the Admiralty.   Meanwhile the rest of
the town, and even the great square, of which this
forms a corner, remain in their usual state of
quiescence.

The streets are never disorderly, partly owing to
the natural mildness of the Russian character; and
partly to the circumstance of a man, dressed in the
coarsest and plainest garb imaginable, standing here
and there with a pole-axe in his hand, to preserve
order.   It is true there is nothing terrible about
these persons but their pole-axes, and they are not
half so much soldiers, either in appearance or reality,
as the "police *force*" of London; but still they are
at least a symbol of authority, and a standing
memento to the passers-by to take care of what they
are about.

These passers-by consist, as in all other cities, of
the upper, middle, and lower classes; for in Russia
there is a middle class in appearance, although none
in reality.   The upper classes, when they ride, are
usually in coaches drawn by four horses, the traces
so long that a single equipage would take up no
inconsiderable part of a street in any other city.
Here, however, they are only in proportion with the
space in which they have to move; a space in which
an English gentleman's carriage, with its two horses,

cocking up their poor, maimed, miserable tails under the coachman's feet, would look mean and ridiculous.

The English, however, although they have the bad taste and brutality to amputate their horses' tails, are the best coachmakers in the world. The carriages of Russia, principally made by German workmen, are inferior even to those of France. The traces, at least in St. Petersburg, are always of leather, but rarely clean, and never polished. The coachman is dressed in a caftan, reaching to his heels, generally blue, and confined at the waist with a red sash. His neck is bare, except where it is covered in front by a handsome beard; and his head is surmounted by a small, low, sturdy-looking hat, considerably broader at the crown than at the brim. The postillion is a dwarfish urchin, dressed in the same fashion, and perched like a cock-sparrow upon one of the fore horses. When the equipage stops, the coachman leans back on his box and goes to sleep; and the postillion descending, lays himself down under the horses' heads, in such a position that they cannot advance without stepping upon his body, and goes to sleep too.

The droski is a still more common equipage: it is the hackney coach of Russia. It consists of a plank of wood, stuffed, and covered with cloth or leather, and hung between two pairs of wheels. On this machine the wayfarer mounts astride, and sits very comfortably—there being a resting place for his feet, defended from the mud by leathern bulwarks—

till the vehicle begins to move. On this consummation taking place, all is misery. The springs are bad, the pavement hideous; and the tyro in such travelling, curses by his gods the infernal apparatus. But at a season of the year like this there is no alternative. He must employ a droski, or remain at home; for although the trottoirs are tolerable, the crossings of the streets are altogether impracticable.

The driver is rarely, if ever, provided with a whip. He holds the bridle in both hands, that are widely separated, and extended before him; and at the seldom time when he finds occasion, employs the end of the "ribbons" for the admonition of his horse. In general he occupies the same plank, only straddling a little in advance of his fare; but sometimes there is a small coach-box for his special use. In either case, the gentleman-passenger, if he has a grain of sensibility, is ashamed of the scurvy figure he cuts, sitting, with his little pig-tailed coat, and naked chin, behind a full flowing caftan, and a manly beard. The military, however, are not unworthy of such an honour. An officer in the army, sitting behind an *isvoschik*, flying at the rate of ten miles an hour, with his ample grey cloak, distended at the shoulders by the epaulettes beneath, his cocked hat, and long feather floating behind, forms one of the most picturesque and characteristic spectacles to be seen in St. Petersburg.

The pedestrians, independently of the class of ladies and gentlemen common to all Europe, are the native merchants, whom I have termed the middle

classes, and the artizans and country people. The
merchants have in general laid aside the sash, but
the beard still flourishes, and the caftan still flows.
Their wives are dressed in rich silk cloaks, lined
with fur, yet with nothing on the head but a very
small handkerchief. But artizans and labourers,
with their sheepskin tunics, or omni-coloured caftans,
their shirt of every gaudy hue worn over their
trowsers, their long boots, or rag-stockings and shoes
of the linden bark, are assuredly the most interesting
figures of the whole. Their hair is cut round horizontally on a line drawn from about the middle of
the nose, and most of the workmen wear a sort of
chaplet, sometimes studded with little pieces of
metal like the ornaments of a horse, to prevent it
from falling into their eyes. In their sash are stuck
their gloves, indispensable for eight months in the year,
and their short-handled, large-bladed axe, which to
a Russian artificer answers the purpose of almost
every tool.

You never see these men in a hurry. There is a
measured gravity about all their motions which adds
to the orientalism of their appearance. They look
as if they were conscious of wearing a beard. The
labourers generally appear in groups; for the use
of machinery is an innovation to which they have not
as yet submitted. If a heavy article is to be moved,
it is dragged by a dozen, a score, or a hundred men
as may be requisite. If it is to be raised to the
scaffolding of a house, it is rolled up an inclined
plane constructed of planks for the purpose. Pul-

leys and blocks are looked upon as a sacrilegious
interference with the evident intentions of nature
and the rights of man.   The same simplicity appears
in their tools.   The carpenter demands nothing more
besides his axe, than a kind of rude chisel and a
gimlet.   His measure is a bit of wood which he
picks up among the chips, or slices off at the
moment from the nearest plank.

Even in that simple but troublesome apparatus,
which is requisite to enable plasterers and painters
to perform their operations on the outside surface of
a building, the Russians usually prefer risking life
and limb to the multiplication of machinery.   Their
ladder frequently consists of a single pole, instead of
two, furnished with transverse bars of wood for steps;
and this pole is occasionally used not only as a
ladder but as a support for a small stage, at one and
the same time.   When it is necessary to move a
ladder of this kind, the workman disdains to descend
for so simple a purpose.   He places himself astride,
near the top, on one of the transverse bars, and
shoving the machine from the wall, leaps with it, so
to speak, to the required distance.   At the same
instant, a comrade below, watching his manœuvres,
moves adroitly the foot of the ladder, and the hero
escapes being precipitated to the ground by an inch
of space and an instant of time.

Sometimes, however, the removal of the apparatus
is inconvenient, or the stage is found to be too low
to enable him to reach the top of the wall: but
these difficulties do not induce a true Russian to be

guilty of the folly of expending time in the construction of one edifice for the purpose of painting or stuccoing another. In this case, the wanderer of St. Petersburg, if he chance to turn up his eyes, sees a pole projected from the roof of the house in question, with a man lying all his length upon it, head downwards. If you marvel at the calm gravity with which the workman thus circumstanced uses his brush or his trowel under the eaves, you are told there is little or no danger, as a friend behind is doing him the kindness to hold him by the heels.

During the intervals of labour, these men, like the coachmen and postillions, go to sleep wherever they happen to leave off work. But still, as if by a kind of natural perversity, they choose such situations for their repose, as seem the least adapted in the world for such a purpose. A mason, for instance, does not lay himself down under the lee of one of the immense blocks of marble or granite on which he is working : he poises himself upon the extreme edge of the mass. Or, if there is a marshy place in the immediate neighbourhood (for he will not trouble himself to go far in search of it) he disposes of his body in instalments upon the stones, or planks, which protrude from the mud. Sometimes the parapet of a bridge is the chosen couch ; sometimes the outer ledge ; but if a piece of wood projects from the steps of the quay over, or upon, the river, this is too tempting an opportunity for indulgence to be missed on any account.

The mujik in St. Petersburgh, however, is a

solitary animal, so far as the women are concerned, and perhaps to this may be owing his habitual gravity. In spring he comes from his village far in the interior—perhaps many hundred miles, and in autumn returns to his family with his little earnings. Each class of labourers comes from a particular government, often from a particular district in that government; and hence in the city they appear to form so many distinct tribes. The finer sort of work, however, is always intrusted to foreigners. The joiners, for instance, may be Russians, but the cabinet-makers are Germans. No nobleman would condescend to have his clothes made by a countryman of his own, or to eat of bread that was baked by native fingers. An exception, however, is made, in one respect, in favour of the fair sex. The wet nurses are taken from the peasantry, and are distinguished in the streets by a kind of lofty crown, generally covered with gold lace. The waists of these women are scarcely shorter than usual, and yet the bosom is beneath, rather than above the girdle. This extraordinary perversity of taste—for the geography of nature is thus outraged systematically from their earliest youth—we shall find, on leaving St. Petersburg, to be common to the female peasantry of the whole of Great Russia.

In most other European cities, the upper and lower classes are but little distinguished from each other in dress, except by the quality of the materials; or in manners, except by the degrees of refinement or vulgarity. Here they form, to all appearance, two separate and distinct races. Elsewhere the common people are partakers in the civilization of the gentry; they follow their steps, at a greater or less distance, in education and knowledge; and are, to all intents and purposes, members of the same family of man. Here, on the contrary, there is hardly one idea in common between the two classes. This is the grand distinctive feature in St. Petersburg. This is the peculiarity in the Russian empire which makes it the most curious, and, to the philosopher, the most interesting, spectacle presented to-day in Europe.

The cause of all the anomalies exhibited by the country may be traced to the suddenness with which civilization took its rise, and the celerity of its progress. The great majority of the nation were in that state of barbarous dependence from which England, for instance, only emerged after many centuries of struggles. The nobles were awakened all on a sudden to a consciousness of their situation with regard to the rest of Europe. A re-action in their feelings even took place; and from the extreme of barbarous pride and ignorant intolerance, they rushed at once to the opposite extreme of liberality. Strangers, who formerly travelled in their country with as much difficulty and danger as in China, were received with acclamations, and loaded with gifts and distinctions. They threw open their churches, which had hitherto been hermetically sealed against heretics; and even permitted temples of every possible religion to flourish by the side of their own. They travelled abroad, for the first time, to see that world

which they had so long contemplated only through
the mists of prejudice; and imitating, or transplant-
ing, whatever struck their imaginations most, they
began to build a new Rome among the snows of the
North.

The mass of the people, in the meantime—the
cultivators of the fields, the hewers of wood, and the
drawers of water—could not possibly remain unin-
fluenced by this spirit of revolution. A corresponding change took place among the peasantry.
Ambition and pride were generated where nothing
of the kind ever existed before; and to this moment,
every day, every hour, some individuals are detaching
themselves from the mass, and rising into the rights
and privileges of freemen. This is provided for by
the laws of the country; and this consummation, it
is well known to all persons possessing information
on the subject, is not only the earnest desire, but the
obvious personal policy of the Emperor. In a future
chapter I shall offer some remarks on the nature and
extent of the change; but at present it will only be
necessary to suggest, in reply to an anticipated
question, that the *peasants* of Russia form a mass
of about *fifty millions*, and that, setting every
extraneous obstacle out of the question, the progress, both moral and political, of such a body is
necessarily much slower than that of a body of a
few hundred thousand. Supposing that a number
of the peasantry equal to that of the whole body of
nobility has been raised, in so short a space of time,
to the benefits of civilization—and the number is

much greater—still, in so vast a population, this must be imperceptible on a superficial view, and the distinction between the two classes of society must remain, to all appearance, as broad as ever.

But with regard to our immediate affairs, St. Petersburg is a city of the nobles, built at their own cost, and according to their own taste. The common people either burrow in their shops under the dwellings of the great, or live, in the usual dirt and crowd, in the hollow squares formed by the houses—for of course all the exterior must be clean, and showy, and glittering to the eye. As for the mujiks from the interior, who give so much of the foreign and picturesque to the show, they are only birds of passage, who come hither to pick up a few crumbs from the abundance generated by the wealth and wants of a great metropolis.

CHAPTER VI.

The Nevski Prospekt—droskis and kibitkas—the troika—
hero of the popular songs—emblem of the Holy Ghost—
catholics and protestants—Armenian worship—remains of
paganism—monks—popes—manners of the clergy—doc-
trines of the Russo-Greek church—the seven sacraments—
marriage—predestination—ceremonies for the dead—secta-
rians and their curious tenets—Kazan church or cathedral
of St. Petersburg—exterior—singularity of the plan—
magnificent colonnade — interior — distinctions of rank
unknown in the temple—where the Spirit of the Lord is
there is liberty.

The day after my initiative stroll through the
city being Sunday, I resolved to devote a portion of
it to the object of acquiring some notions relative
to the churches and religious customs of the place.

Betaking myself to the great square of the
Admiralty, as to the centre from which all things
proceed, and to which all things return, in St.
Petersburg, I launched myself into the Nevski
Prospekt, that great street which has been already
so often mentioned. It is one of several avenues
which radiate from the Admiralty, the gilded spire
of which is seen along the vista, and serves so well
as a beacon, that nobody can be out of his bearings

The Nevskoï Prospect.

St Petersburg

Drawn by A.G. Vickers.

Engraved by S. Fisher.

Printed by Claude Fisher.

London, Published Oct.r 1 1835, for the Proprietors by Longman, & C.º Paternoster Row. Kittner & C.º Paris, & Asher Berlin.

for many minutes together. The view annexed,
looking downwards towards the Admiralty, gives an
idea of the magnitude of this great artery of population, which is very nearly two miles and a half long.

The avenue of trees on either side is refreshing to
the eye, although as yet destitute of shade. On the
right hand in the engraving, beside the group of
peasants, is a droski, but the driver has not been
fortunate enough to obtain a fare. On the left hand
is a vehicle called a kibitka, which is frequently
used for travelling with post-horses. It is without
springs, and being constructed entirely of wood, and
in the most simple manner, may be repaired at any
village on the road. This is its only advantage over
the more comfortable and more aristocratic britchka.

The three horses by which this vehicle is drawn,
are called the Troika, or the three, a name familiar
to all travellers who pause in their journey to listen
to the songs of the people. The post-master does
not keep horses himself, but in obedience to the
printed requisition handed by the traveller, hires
them from the neighbouring peasants; and the
individual they send with them to drive, is of course
the liveliest young fellow in their family. If the
Troika drivers were professional post-boys, there
would be nothing poetical connected with the name;
but they are the flower of the peasantry, and are
further distinguished from the others by enjoying, or
suffering, a greater proportion of the vicissitudes of
life. Without recollecting this, the traveller will
wonder at the taste which selects such heroes for

the popular ballads, and lays the scene in an inn court, or on the highway. The highways, too, it should be remembered, are not a little romantic themselves; being in general nothing more than wild and savage tracks formed only by carriage wheels and horses' feet.

Keeping these considerations in view, even the most fastidious listener will hear sometimes with interest the fortunes of his postillion, commencing in a strain like this :—

> " Away, away, along the road,
> The gallant Troika bound,
> While 'neath the dooga, sadly sweet,
> Their Valdai bells resound."

The dooga is a sort of bow which arches over the neck of the middle horse, and with which almost all the Russian vehicles are provided. A bell is generally suspended from this bow, and those mentioned in the above stanza of a popular song are made at Valdai, a village on the Moscow road celebrated for the manufacture.

But the engraving presents another peculiarity more germane to the matter of the present chapter. It is a flock of pigeons—an indispensable part of a street view in this country. The pigeon is in some sense the Redbreast of Russia; but he is protected by a higher and holier prestige than poor Robin. To kill, or insult, a pigeon is an act of sacrilege as well as immorality; it is, in fact, to lift the hand against the third person of the Trinity—for the dove is the emblem of the Holy Ghost.

A Catholic chapel attracted my attention first, as I journeyed along churchward; but, accustomed as I have been in other countries to the great temples of this modification of the Christian faith, I saw nothing in it worthy of remark. The congregation, however, was numerous and devout—two circumstances which rarely occur in what are called Catholic countries. In Ireland, where the Protestant is the "dominant" religion, the Catholics are as *devout* in their way as they were several centuries ago. This may arise from the fact, that they are that space of time behind the civilized world in civilization; but how shall we account for the Protestantism of Ireland being at this moment identical in spirit, with that of the most ignorant and ferocious epoch in our history? The strange thing is, that even those English Protestants, who take a part in Irish disputes, become embued all at once with the same fanaticism! This is what the Catholics of the continent (with the exception of those of Spain and Portugal) cannot comprehend. They listen with shouts of laughter to our quarrels about the pope; but when they hear of our actually cutting throats for conscience' sake, they are ready to conclude, that in spite of our excellence in cotton-spinning, and the extreme dexterity at which we have arrived in blowing people up into the air with steam-engines, we are still at bottom, Protestants and Catholics, a race of stupid and unteachable barbarians.

I

An Armenian church, almost next door, soon invited my attention, and I was surprised, I do not know why, to find less devotion among the congregation than I ever witnessed in my life in a religious assembly. The genteel part of the audience consisted of a small number of ladies apart from the men; and although they performed the same kind of genuflections and prostrations that are customary in the Greek church, these were so openly intermingled with nodding, whispering, and giggling, that the one might have seemed as much a part of the ceremony as the other.

A young Armenian lady, whom I had the pleasure to meet with afterwards at Moscow, explained this oddity, or at least apologized for it, in a very intelligent manner.

"Although Armenians by descent," said she, "we are born in Russia, and intermingled from our birth with Russian society. We thus lose very soon, if indeed we ever acquire, the language of our country; for it has no beauty, and no literature, to make it worth retaining. How, then, can you expect us to take an interest in the services of our church, hardly one word of which we comprehend, and which have nothing beyond the splendour of the priest's vestments to attract attention—but on the contrary, as you must have observed yourself, are dull, drowsy, and monotonous to the last degree that is supportable by human patience?"

This description of the service is exact, and my only wonder is, that the Armenians do not attach themselves to the Russo-Greek church, the form of worship in which is nearly the same, and the language at least a little more intelligible. As for the dogmas of their faith, they are like thoseof every other sect of Christianity I know of, when fairly reported: very little, if at all, repugnant to human reason, and easily proved by the letter of Scripture. As I am now approaching the Kazan church, which is the grand cathedral of St. Petersburg, and where the external service presents nothing to the stranger but the grossest and most stupid idolatry, perhaps the reader—supposing him to be unacquainted with the subject—would like to know what the Russians really do believe.

It is sufficiently well known, although somehow or other in speculations concerning Russia the thing is always forgotten, that the Eastern and Western churches were in the very zenith of their barbarous pride, when this nation *began* to be converted from the darkest heathenism to Christianity. It was not, in fact, till the eleventh century, till the *close* of the iron age in the rest of Europe, that the Christian church took root in Russia. Civilization began as usual to follow even so impure a Christianity as could be obtained from the poisoned fountains of that day—and then the Tatar invasion came, to impose a yoke even upon the minds of men, and arrest the moral progress of the country. It was the middle of the *sixteenth century* before this incubus was thrown off; and it was not till the accession of the present dynasty, in 1613, that any

attempt was made to cleanse the Temple of the
ruins of so many ages of darkness and terror—ruins
in the shade of which the people had reclined so
long, that they had come to look upon them as essential parts of the building.

In the "Spiritual Regulation" promulgated by
Peter the Great, we have evidence of the state of
the church in Russia, which cannot be disputed;
and which is exceedingly interesting as showing
that many remnants of paganism existed even in the
seventeenth century.

The Spiritual College is directed, in that curious
performance, "to compare the history of saints,
whether some of them are not lying devices, or fabu-
lous and ridiculous stories." Such things are the
rather to be discountenanced, "since especially
the simple folk can scarce distinguish the right hand
from the left, but firmly and pertinaciously maintain whatever they see written in a book." The
superstition, also, is condemned which forbids working on Friday, "because Panitsa will be angry."
This personage appears to resemble the Venus of the
heathen; and, even in the ecclesiastical processions
of Little Russia, she walked at that time in the
guise of a woman with dishevelled hair, and was
led into the churches, and exposed for the worship
of the people.

It was believed, according to the same authority,
that a man buried in the Pecherskoi monastery
should be saved, even if he had died impenitent. In
another place, it was the custom to pray before

an oak; and the pope, or priest, in blessing the people, shook the boughs over their heads. The college was especially directed to inquire into the "infinite number of fables" about holy relics; and the conduct of bishops was loudly condemned, who, when in want of money, placed an image in a desert, and persuaded the people that it wrought miracles.

Although this state of the church, however, resembled so much that of Catholicism in the darker ages, the manners of the priesthood were modified by the peculiar position in which they were placed, and by the character of the nation.

The upper clergy, being all monks of St. Basil, and eligible to the highest offices in the church, were taken exclusively from the better classes; and they were true "lords spiritual," with only the usual faults of their order—pride and ambition. As a specimen of the height to which these qualities had attained, it may be mentioned that an annual procession took place on Palm-Sunday, in which the horse of the patriarch was led by the bridle by the Tsar in person, in his imperial robes and crown. At the close of the ceremony, the priest presented the monarch with two hundred rubles for his trouble.

"The bishop," says the regulation of Peter the Great, "ought to command his servants to behave them orderly and soberly in the cities and monasteries which he visits, and to commit no outrage; especially not to exact from monks and popes too great a quantity of meat and drink for themselves, or of provender for their horses; especially that they attempt not to rob, on the pain of being severely chastised: for the servants of bishops are usually a dissolute herd; and when they observe their lord to have any authority, like wild Tatars, they impudently fall to pillage."

At the time of Peter the Great, the spiritual pride engendered by such power became so troublesome that, on the death of the patriarch Adrian, in 1700, instead of appointing a successor, he named, pro tempore, an exarch, or viceregent. Having thus felt his way, he allowed the office to drop altogether, appointing in lieu the Holy Synod, of which he constituted himself the president; thus becoming, like the King of England, the head of the national church. As for the high clergy, they murmured very little. Carried on by the stream of civilization, they are now, like other persons of their class; but with this difference, that, being monks, they do not mix in general society.

The lower clergy,—the priests, or popes, as they are called,—are not only permitted, but enjoined to marry, and they are ineligible to the higher offices. This being the case, they, of course, originate from the peasantry, and their vices are those of the vulgar. Their duty requires only the arts of reading and writing; the sacred language is Slavonian, little different from the dialect of the common people; and their families being intermixed with those of other persons of the same origin and station, they belong essentially to the inferior order of society. Earlier travellers, who are surprised at "the degraded state of the church," forget these circumstances. The character they give of the popes is precisely the character they give of the common people, and it must necessarily be so.

By the "Spiritual Regulation" already quoted, I find it was the custom for the choristers to sing several hymns at the same instant by way of saving time ; and for priests, when summoned by sick persons of little consideration, to send them their prayers—in the hat of the messenger !

" A preacher has no need to tug and heave as though he were tugging at the oar in a boat. He has no need to clap his hands, to set his arms a-kimbo, nor to bounce or spring, nor to giggle and laugh, nor any reason for howlings and hideous lamentations." Surely, this beats Hamlet's directions to the players !

It was a very common custom for men to marry in fits of drunkenness ; and, in cases of this kind, the repentant sinners were admonished not to presume to espouse a second wife till they had laid the disaster before a pope : " *but if the priest himself,*" goes on the Regulation, " *happen to be in the same predicament,* the matter must go before the Spiritual College."

Many, it seems, thrust themselves into priests' orders for no other reason than to revel and debauch with impunity ; and the bishop was especially desired to ascertain, before ordaining priests, that they were not superstitious, nor vagrants, nor hucksters of saints.* Further, "they are not only to observe whether priests and deacons, and the lower ecclesiastics, frequent the stews, or, being drunk, hollow in the streets, or, what is worse, in their drink whoop and hollow in the church, &c., but, what is intolerably shameful, whether they fight in the *boi-kulachni.*" This climax of immorality was a sort of sparring match with gloves fought in the streets, of which the peasants were till lately extremely fond.

Such were the manners of the peasants and the peasant-priests a very short time ago. During three months which I spent in Great Russia, frequenting industriously every kind of assembly of the people, I did not see above half a dozen instances of intoxication; and I never, on any occasion, saw an ecclesiastic otherwise than respectable either in his dress or conduct. This, however, is the progress of civilization unconnected with religion. A priest is not the more esteemed because he is sober; and he is no more admitted now than he was formerly to the tables of the upper classes.

The Russo-Greek church believes in the doctrine of the Trinity, but differs from the Catholic with regard to what is called the procession of the Holy Ghost. The Holy Ghost, according to it, is derived

---

* These persons were dealers in the pictures of saints, which they were permitted to dispose of by way of barter, but not to sell for money. Late travellers say, that this restriction is still in force; but I saw no difference in such respect, even in the " Holy City," Moscow, between the god-market and the fish-market.

from the Father alone, and not from the Father and Son united ; a question that has been fiercely and abundantly argued ; and one very important, no doubt, to the casuists.

The invocation of saints is enjoined, as mediators, subordinate to Christ; and the use of pictures permitted, for the sake of the ignorant, and to assist the devotion of all. This "permission," however, it must be observed, has nothing to do with the essentials of the religion. The well-informed altogether disapprove of such baubles; and, even in the time of Peter the Great, his Synod petitioned to have them taken down from the walls of the churches. Peter, however, daring as he was, did not venture on such a step—it was as much as his crown and life were worth. Nicon, the patriarch, was destroyed by his interference with the gods of the people; although it went only the length of correcting a most laughable abuse.

It was the custom at that time for pictures to be brought to the churches, and nailed to the walls by private individuals, who still, however, insisted upon retaining a spiritual property in the god. They placed him there merely that he might enjoy a suitable temple, and had no notion of his dispensing his favours to other people. When they detected a neighbour, therefore, in the fact of adoring him, they were indignant at the dishonesty; curses and revilings were sometimes followed by severer vengeance ; and they even sought to recover damages for the pious roguery in the courts of law.

These pictures were at length got rid of, on account of the scandal they caused; and the more enlightened party in the church consoled themselves with the idea, that those which they were still obliged to endure did not come within the meaning of the second commandment, not being *graven images*.

The mysteries, or sacraments, are seven in number.

Baptism takes place on the eighth day, and is held to be so important, that if a priest cannot be got in time, it may be administered by any body, and it is never, on any account whatever, to be repeated.

Chrism is an anointing with oil immediately after baptism, and is called "the seal of the gift of the Holy Ghost." The priest, in anointing the child, makes the sign of the cross on his forehead, eyes, nostrils, mouth, ears, breast, hands, and feet, saying each time, "the seal of the gift of the Holy Ghost." The child's hair is then cut cross-wise, the priest wrapping up some locks in wax, and throwing them into the font. In seven days the new Christian is brought back, and is publicly washed by the priest.

In the Eucharist the doctrine of Transubstantiation is held. The wine, however, must be mixed with warm water, the bread sopped in the liquid, and both given together with a spoon. The priests, however, take the elements separately. The napkin spread upon the holy table must be consecrated by a bishop, and must have some small particle of the reliques of a martyr mixed in the web.

The other sacraments are, Confession, Ordination, Marriage, and the Holy Oil, or Extreme Unction.

Marriage is divided into two parts, now usually performed consecutively, the Espousals, and the Matrimonial Coronation. At the former, the priest places rings upon the fingers of the two parties, with many prayers, and the paranymphus exchanges them from one to the other. At the latter, the priest crowns them (formerly with flowers, now with a silver or tin crown belonging to the church), saying, " The servant of God—is crowned for the handmaid of God—in the name of the Father, the Son, and the Holy Ghost." The mutual cup is then given; and, walking three times in a circle, their crowns are taken off, and they salute each other. In eight days they return to the church, and their crowns are " dissolved " by prayer.

The doctrine of predestination, which has so remarkable an effect on the Russian character, is pretty nearly the same as the dogma in the seventeenth article of the Anglican church.

The prayers and service for the dead are merely a kind of commemoration of departed friends. There is no purgatory, no indulgence, no dispensations. When a Russian dies, the priest comes and reads a service over the body ; but in the case of a wealthy person, a succession of priests and clerks read the gospel and psalter all the time it remains in the house, night and day. Funerals always take place in the morning, and the mourners kiss either the body or the coffin. It was formerly the custom to provide this mute traveller with a pair of shoes for the journey, or a white handkerchief to wipe his face after arrival. These observances are now done away with; although in the Swedish provinces I believe it is still usual among the peasantry to put a piece of money into the coffin. As for the *passport* with which the dead is furnished by the priest, the story has been refuted so often as to make it hardly necessary to say, that the paper contains merely a prayer and confession of faith.

Some of the Russian dissenters are peculiarly wild in their notions. One sect forbids application to worldly labour, that its members may always be ready to receive the Holy Ghost when it comes. There is another in which each man baptizes himself, from an idea that there is no one left on earth holy enough to perform the office. Some think that Anti-Christ is come, and has put an end to all righteousness in the church; others consider it meritorious to terminate their lives by fasting: but the most numerous are the Old Ceremonialists and the Anti-Ceremonialists—those who wish to incorporate the rites of Judaism with the doctrine of the New Testament, and those who wish to deprive Christianity of every external form whatever.

The Anti-Ceremonialists, who have, to a certain extent, existed in all Christian countries in one shape or other, are the descendants, as they inform us, of Shadrach, Meshach, and Abednego, the three "children" who were thrown into the fire because they would not fall down and worship the golden image of Nebuchadnezzar. They will have no ikons, no ceremonies, no churches, no appointed days ; for all times, all places, are alike holy. They meet in one another's houses and sup together, like Christ and his disciples ; praying, singing hymns, and expounding the Word. The women preach as well as the men ; and when they pray, they pray standing, or sitting, or kneeling, or lying, just as fancy, convenience, or accident directs, for all postures are alike holy.

They possess all things in common ; and the only punishment they inflict is expulsion from their society. If any one seeks this voluntarily—even if a wife wishes to leave her husband, or a husband his wife, they give them a share of the public property, and bid them go in peace. The history of the Saviour is entirely symbolical : it has no meaning but in a spiritual sense. He must be begotten in us, be born in us, grow up in us, teach in us, suffer in us, die in us. Baptism is identical with regeneration, and it takes place inwardly. The Communion is received when the Word of God, which is Christ, sinks into the heart ; and as for bread and wine, it is absurd to suppose that this can be of use to any thing but the body.

Fasting from food is folly : to abstain from sin is the true fast of the righteous. Marriage is not a sacrament : it is merely a verbal contract, by which a man and a woman promise to live together.

K

When seduction takes place, and the promise implied by it remains unfulfilled, the recusant party is expelled. Death is merely a change, and is no subject for mourning. The good will be rewarded and the bad punished in a future life.

After this brief review of the religion of the country, we may proceed with our as hasty glances at the churches of St. Petersburg. In ascending the Nevski Prospekt, we arrive at a superb semicircular colonnade, surmounted in the middle by a comparatively pigmy dome. This is the Kazan church, the cathedral of the city, and in some respects one of the most beautiful modern buildings in Europe. In the view, in which the reader will admire the consummate skill of the artist, a bridge, on the opposite side of the street is interposed, without impairing the effect of the principal object.

The body of the church lies parallel with the Nevski Prospekt, in the form of a Latin cross; and thus one of the arms is towards the street, or towards the reader in the engraving. This was not the fault of the architect, for it was necessary that the altar should point to the east; and yet, for the sake of the architecture of the city, it was also necessary that the grand façade should face the street. Disregarding, for this reason, the form of the edifice, Veronikhin boldly attached his colonnade to the northern arm of the cross; where, therefore, is the great door of the church, approached through the majestic avenue of columns, entered at either side by a superb portal.

Drawn by A. G. Vickers.

Engraved by J. T. Willmore.

The Kazan Church and Bridge.

St. Petersburg.

If the relative position of the principal parts of the building could be seen at once from the Nevski, the effect would be destructive of that idea of order which is indispensable in edifices of this kind ; but fortunately, or perhaps intentionally, the columns are so thickly set as almost to conceal the body of the church, and thus there is very little to disturb our impressions of fitness and beauty.

The misfortune is, however, that the architect, while thus changing his plan to suit the nature of the ground, forgot to consider the effect which the alteration would have on the general proportions of the work :—for I cannot help imagining that the columns were an after-thought, suggested not with reference to the church but to the street. The dome, therefore, which would have been somewhat too small at any rate, when viewed as the centre of the vast colonnade becomes altogether ridiculous.

The colonnade is formed of two double rows of Corinthian pillars of polished granite, the bases and capitals of which are of cast iron. The pavement, to which you ascend by steps, is of red granite within the columns, and of grey without. The portico is adorned with a bronze statue at either side, one of the archangel Gabriel, and the other of Michael ; and the door, imitated from that of the Cathedral of Florence, is likewise of bronze, and very beautiful.

But the natural entrance of the building is by the western door, and there the interior presents itself in its greatest magnificence. The vault

is semi-circular, and rests on a gilded cornice,
supported by fifty-six Corinthian columns and
forty pilasters of red granite of enormous size,
and of a polish equal to that of marble. The
bases and capitals of these columns are of burnished
brass; while those of the pilasters, with that
mixture of paltriness and grandeur which is conspicuous throughout the whole city, are made to
correspond—with yellow paint! At the farther
end, the ikonastas sparkles brilliantly with gold
and gems, and pretty faces of female saints looking
out of draperies of gilded metal, richly framed.
The doors and rails are of massive silver. There
are few pictures, and none remarkable for either
merit or demerit.

The dome still appears small, but not nearly so
much so as when viewed from the outside. The
pavement beneath, and, indeed, throughout the
church, is among the most beautiful I have ever
seen, and is entirely formed of the jaspers and
marbles of Olonetz and Siberia. The walls in
different places are hung with banners and other
trophies taken in battle. No description in words,
however, can convey any definite idea of such a
scene, and the pen willingly transfers the task to
the pencil.

In this magnificent temple all who come to
worship stand intermingled. In most other countries the distinctions of human society are as
jealously kept up in the churches as in the
palaces; and there the house of God may truly be

Drawn by A. G. Vickers.

Engraved by T. Higham.

Interior of the Kazan Church.

S.t Petersburg.

Drawn by A. G. Vickers.

Engraved by J. Turnbull.

The Colonnade of the Kazan Church.

St. Petersburg.

London, Published Oct.r 1, 1835, for the Proprietor by Longman & C.o Paternoster Row, Rittner & C.o Paris, Asher, Berlin

Printed by Ormsby & Fisher.

likened to the kingdom of heaven, for in it are
many mansions. Here the lord and the bondman
meet on equal terms, as men and brethren. The
mujik turns his glowing eyes towards the altar
through clouds of matted hair ; some rough sounds
of prayer come in whispers from his lips; and,
falling down upon his face, he strikes the marble
pavement with his forehead. The drapery of
another devotee mingles with his coarse garments
in the crowd; another brow touches the earth on
the same spot; the breath of prayer and praise
from other lips blends with his, and rises to heaven
at the same instant. The drapery is of silk ;
the brow sparkles with gems : his fellow-worshipper
is a princess. The two leave the temple side by
side ; the one as conscious as the other that in
the holy place there is no master but One. At
the door the scene changes instantaneously. They
are again in the world. The princess raises her
haughty head, or bends it with graceful condescen-
sion ; and the poor mujik, clasping his hands upon his
chest, bows his body almost to the earth before her
who but a moment before was his equal and his
sister.

On leaving the Kazan church, I am enabled
to present the reader with a view of a portion of the
colonnade, and one of its portals, which taken in
conjunction with the last engraving, will enable him
to form a good idea of the localities.

CHAPTER VII.

Monastery of Saint Alexander Nevskoi—its origin—singular
colouring—description of the principal church—stupendous
silver shrine of the saint—the cemetery and its monuments—
Russian monks and nuns—the Neva and the Neva water—
Smolnoi monastery—singular mixture of the mean and the
grand—Taurida palace—gigantic hall half a mile in circumference—Catharine II. and Potemkin—Marble palace—the
fortress and the church of Saint Peter and Saint Paul—
extraordinary exploit of a mujik.

THE Nevski Prospekt, setting out from the
Admiralty Square, forms the cord of a bow, or
rather the base of an irregular triangle, made by one
of the windings of the Neva. Its length is nearly
two miles and a half, and during a considerable
portion of this distance it is lined with distinguished
buildings. Towards the end, where it is just about
reaching the river again, stands the Monastery of
Saint Alexander Nevskoi; to whose shrine I bent
my steps after leaving the Kazan church.

Alexander Iaroslavich was Grand Duke of Novgorod in the thirteenth century, and the Swedes
were at that time the "natural enemies" of the
country. In 1241 King Eric the Great sailed up
the Neva in a fleet conveying an army composed of
Swedes and Livonians, the latter being the forces of
the Brothers of the Sword. At the confluence of the
Neva with the Ijora he was met by Alexander, and
totally defeated. The conqueror after his death was
canonized by the church, and received the title of
Nevskoi—Saint Alexander of the Neva—to per-
petuate the memory of his victory.

When Peter the Great had performed similar
exploits at the same place, and against the same
enemies, it is no wonder that he recurred with
profound respect to the memory of Alexander—that
the bones of the Saint were brought with distinguished honour to the banks of the Neva—and that
a rich monastery soon rose upon the spot. Peter,
however, did not remember, nor do I find the fact
alluded to by subsequent writers, that at the epoch
of this victory, although the Russians were fighting
against the Swedes, they were the abject slaves of
the Tatars; and that after Alexander's accession to
the crown, no prince could be more abject than he.

Within the walls of the monastery there are ten
places of worship, although many of them hardly
deserve the name of churches. In three of these
service is regularly performed; and the principal
temple is a very remarkable edifice. It forms the
centre of one side of an almost square figure, the

other side consisting of low buildings which are the
rest of the churches, the palace of the Archbishop of
Kazan, and the cells and halls of the monks.

The façade of the church is chaste and beautiful,
with a simple Doric portico; and above these rise
two thick towers, with a large dome behind. The
towers are ornamented with square, and the dome
with round pilasters; the Corinthian capitals of
which are jet black, while the rest of the building is
snow white! The other sides of the square, with
the exception of the window cases, which are white,
are *blood red!*

On entering the church, however, you forget
these oddities without. It is strikingly elegant, and
wants only more space to be grand. Its form is, on
a small scale, that of the cathedral, but the dome is
better proportioned to the size of the building.
The gates of the ikonastas are of gilded metal, in open
work, richly interspersed with small paintings. The
sanctum, unlike those of the other Greek churches, is
entered also by side avenues patent to the public;
but they disclose little else than the customary pyx
on its ornamented table, surmounted by the peristerium. Behind this is a semicircle of huge columns,
and a painting of little value by Raphael Mengs.

In the open part of the church, on the right as
you face the altar, is the tomb of Saint Alexander,
with a large sarcophagus of silver, sculptured in bas
relief with battle pieces. At each side is a trophy
of military arms, and behind an altar—the whole of
silver. In all this the details are so minute, and

the ornaments so light and numerous, that the
effect is frittered away into mere gaudiness. With
such a prodigious mass of silver to work upon, an
artist of taste would have made one of the most
splendid monuments in the world. A silver chande-
lier, notwithstanding, hanging from the roof near the
door, is a masterpiece of elegance. The columns
throughout the church are handsome, and of as
beautiful marble—as a painter, with a pot of white
and blue paint, can be reasonably expected to
manufacture.

Near this building, there is a small church where
are the monuments of many illustrious Russian
families ; and close by, a churchyard thickly strewn
with the bones of the mighty dead—and of the
mean. The area is small, but so crowded with little
monuments of the ambitious class, that it looks like
a Lilliputian Pere la Chaise. These monuments
consist of columns, urns, sarcophagi, statues, &c.
&c., few of any merit, but all of great pretensions.
Most of the marble and granite of which they are
composed is already splitting and crumbling away ;
as if the friends of the beloved dead had studied
economy in the materials as well as in the execution.

The monks, clad in black robes, with a black veil
hanging down from the back of the cap, look well
fed and respectable. They had a listless and idle
gait, however, like men who were fatigued with
doing nothing. I do not know how far the regulation of Peter the Great was carried into effect,
"that the archimandrite by no means suffer monks

to be idle, but find them some daily business; and it were not amiss to teach them a trade, to wit, joiner's work, or painting of images, and the like, which a monk may be allowed to do; and monkesses, or nuns, to knit, sew, or weave, lace, &c." A few nuns are occasionally seen in St. Petersburg; but these are all from the interior. They stand at the doors of the churches, begging mutely for their convents.

Having left the monastery, instead of returning to the centre of the town by land, I took a boat and descended the Neva. This glorious river is perhaps the only object in St. Petersburg whose beauty and grandeur are wholly unmixed with meanness and bad taste. Even the granite quays, the most magnificent in Europe, seem to be a proof that the architects of the city received a peculiar influence from the genius of the Neva, and were afraid to approach the stream with any thing fantastic or ignoble.

To drink the water of the river is worth a journey to Russia of itself. It is the most delicious draught imaginable, and has besides a medicinal property favourable to most constitutions. Strangers, indeed, are cautioned against using it too freely; but in my own case, although I drank of it almost to excess, I found no *bad* effects whatever. It is found on analysis, to contain much carbonic acid, without any metallic parts except a scarcely perceptible quantity of common salt.

After a pleasant sail, the scene in the opposite

Drawn by A. G. Vickers.

Engraved by J. Appleton.

The Smolnoy Convent.

From the Neva, St. Petersburg.

London, Oct'r 1, 1835. Published for the Proprietor, by Jennings & C'o. Paternoster Row, Rittner & C'o. Paris, & Asher, Berlin.

engraving presented itself, and I was tempted to
land for the purpose of visiting the Smolnoi Monastery. This building is seen at a great distance, and
the voyager on the river is tantalized by its apparent
propinquity long before he approaches it. The body
of the edifice resembles a single tower of enormous
thickness, surmounted by one large dome, and four
small onion-shaped cupolas, all glittering with golden
stars on a blue ground, and their spires, or spikes,
covered with golden ornaments. The effect notwithstanding is far from being vulgar; for the temple
is as white as snow, and all this finery is in keeping.

I observed here a very curious instance of the
mixture of the mean and gorgeous, which I have
noticed in a greater or less degree in almost all the
public buildings of the metropolis. A balustrade
runs round the top of the main building, at least
in front, and appears to form part of the stonework.
This, however, is nothing else than a thin board,
painted and shaded so as to resemble the bulb-
shaped rails common in similar works. Having
ascertained that I was not mistaken, it occurred
to me that this strange ornament might have
been put up in a temporary manner, merely
with the view of trying the effect; but, unfortunately, it exactly corresponds in apparent age and
colour with the rest of the edifice.

The interior was undergoing some repairs which
prevented me from entering; but I understand it
presents nothing remarkable. From this main
point, vast curving wings extend at either side, till

they almost meet at a considerable distance from the
body of the edifice.   The whole is now occupied by
the Communauté des Demoiselles Nobles, an establishment of education already amply described by
former travellers.

As the winding of the Neva at this place presented nothing of interest, I dismissed my boat,
and walked onwards from the monastery in a
straight line for nearly half a mile.   I was here
arrested by the appearance of a building fronting
the river at a little distance from the brink, with
a very long, low façade, a simple Doric portico, and
a large dome.   This I was told was the Taurida
Palace ; and very different, indeed, did it appear,
from the gigantic associations that were connected
in my mind with the name.

On entering, however, I was completely re-
assured ; and I felt that the eulogiums of travellers,
however incorrect in detail, were not exaggerated
with regard to effect.   The vestibule of the grand
hall is a circular apartment, with the dome for its
roof, supported by white columns.   From this you
pass into the hall itself, not by a door, but between
the columns, and a scene opens, such as probably
the visitor never before beheld, and never will
again.

The hall, at the side of which you enter, is two
hundred and fifty-one feet long, the roof supported
by sixty-four columns of the Roman Ionic, more
than ten feet in circumference.   These columns are
disposed in a double row running along each side ;

but, when your eye comes to calculate the breadth, it loses itself in an area beyond the opposite row as great as the one within. These two spaces have been described by travellers as the Hall and the Winter Garden; but, in reality, they form a single gigantic apartment, only divided by the pillars that were necessary to support the roof. The breadth of the whole, from the vestibule to the farther side of the Winter Garden, is one hundred and sixty-seven feet. To go round this apartment, therefore, is to walk within forty-four yards of half a mile!

The ceiling unfortunately is flat. A vaulted roof, or, rather, two vaults meeting at the columns, would have made the Taurida Palace not merely grand and noble, but sublime. Storch says, that the columns are under the form of palm-trees, which is a mistake. In the compartment called the Winter Garden there are poles placed among the trees, surmounted by crimson-coloured glass lamps; but the "extensiveness" of this garden, and its "winding and undulating walks," are manifestly exaggerations, altogether uncalled for. The "magnificent lustres of cut-glass," described by travellers, have now dwindled into chandeliers of wood, ornamented with tin leaves; and the silken curtains, festoons, and mirrors, mentioned by Tooke, have altogether disappeared. The Garden is not semi-circular, as this writer asserts, but of the same form as the Hall, only *wanting* the semi-circular ends. The statues still exist, and are in general indifferent copies of the antique; and in the vesti-

L

bule may still be seen, "mingled," as Sir Robert Ker Porter says, "in monstrous association—modern ill-fashioned Cupids, negroes, fantastic heads, and hideous pedestals of fifty-coloured marble."

This palace was built by Catharine II. for her lover Potemkin ; and it was here he gave a feast to his imperial mistress, which has been often described. On this occasion, the illustrious savage was on the pinnacle of his glory, beyond which hope itself could not soar. Catharine, enchanted with the wonders of the scene, and desiring to evidence her friendship for its master, had remained long after her usual time of retiring from public. On a new swell of music, as a hymn to her own praise burst upon her ear, she turned round in emotion to the prince. Potemkin sank upon his knees, seized her hand, and wept.

They were, perhaps, the first tears which those proud and stern eyes had ever shed. But now, all was accomplished : his destiny was fulfilled ; he felt as if he had lived long enough. He left St. Petersburgh soon after, with a presentiment that he should never return. At the Congress of Yassy he was attacked with an epidemical fever ; and, on leaving that place, he alighted from his carriage in the middle of the road, laid himself down under a tree, and died.

In proceeding to the centre of the city in a straight line from the Taurida Palace, the next remarkable building which arrested my progress was the Marble Palace.

Mr. Rae Wilson says of this palace, that it may be ranked in point of elegance next to the imperial one : but the imperial one, he tells us, is " by no means an elegant specimen of architecture." Other writers, however, are more complimentary. Its grandeur, they say, is unparalleled in Europe; and Tooke declares its magnificence to be such, " that it never fails to remind the beholder who sees it for the first time, of what he has read in the Arabian Nights, fairy and genii tales, and the like."

This edifice forms three sides of a quadrangle, the central one surmounted by a sort of belfry, with a clock. The door is small, mean, and paltry, to the last degree, and certainly would not be considered at all ornamental to a respectable private house. The lower story is of granite, and the superstructure of grey marble, adorned with columns of red marble. Were it not for the door, however, which is singularly poor, it might justly be termed, on a front view, a handsome building : but I cannot say more.

The windows are unusually flat, the glass being very little removed from the surface of the wall; and this, together with the form of the edifice, makes it appear, when viewed from any other direction than the front, like a huge, square box. In the interior, every thing is petite. The entrance-hall is not so spacious as that of most gentlemen's houses ; the multiplicity of columns and statues there, and on the stairs, rather injures the effect than otherwise. These are of marble, and the walls scagliola, but the latter so much injured from damp and neglect as to look like common plaster.

The hall and staircase are entire; the rest of the interior ruins. I ascended without any other interruption than a stare of inquiry and surprise from the sentries stationed with fixed bayonets in the court and at the door; and the flapping of wings above my head proclaimed that doves, if not owls, now roosted in the chambers of princes.

During the reign of Paul, the Marble Palace was inhabited by the King of Poland till his death. I am only surprised that the progress of decay has been so rapid in so short a time.

It is rather odd that the front of so costly a building should not have been made to face the river, close to which it stands. The view from this spot is very fine; and the Fortress directly in front, on the opposite side, appeared so tempting to my curiosity, that I took boat and embarked again.

As a fortress, this place can be of no practical utility; but its strong walls, notwithstanding, rising from the water's edge, serve to give a military character to the scene. The church of Saint Peter and Saint Paul within the precincts, is remarkable as containing the tombs of the emperors; and it is also remarkable for its spire, the loftiest in St. Petersburg.

The opposite view is taken from a point where the Exchange stands; a corner of which building you observe on the left, with one of the rostral columns. Just beyond this column, an arm of the

Drawn by A. G. Vickers.

Engraved by J. T. Willmore.

The Fortress and Church of St. Peter and St. Paul.

from the Iron Bridge, St. Petersburg.

London, Oct.r 1, 1836. Published for the Proprietor by Longman & Co. Paternoster Row, Hinton & C.o Paris, & Asher, Berlin.

river sweeps past the Exchange, to enter speedily
the Gulf of Finland; and in front, at some distance,
rising from the main body of the stream, but near
the bank, is seen the fortress, and the tall, slender
spire of Saint Peter and Saint Paul. An anecdote
connected with this church, and not yet known,
I believe, out of Russia, is too remarkable to be
omitted. It places in a conspicuous point of view
that spirit of almost absurd daring which I have
already mentioned as one of the peculiarities of the
national character ; and, in fact, the incident could
not, I think, by possibility, have occurred in any
other country.

The spire, which rises—

  " ———— lofty, and light, and small,"

and is properly represented in the engraving as
fading away almost into a point in the sky, is, in
reality, terminated by a globe of considerable dimensions, on which an angel stands, supporting a
large cross. This angel, less respected by the
weather than perhaps his holy character deserved,
fell into disrepair; and some suspicions were enter-
tained that he designed re-visiting, uninvoked, the
surface of the earth. The affair caused some un-
easiness, and the government at length became
seriously perplexed. To raise a scaffolding to such
a height would have cost more money than all the
angels out of heaven were worth; and, meditating
fruitlessly on these circumstances, without being

able to resolve how to act, a considerable time was suffered to elapse.

Among the crowd of gazers below, who daily turned their eyes and their thoughts towards the angel, was a mujik called Telouchkine. This man was a roofer of houses (a slater, as he would be called in a country where slates are used), and his speculations by degrees assumed a more practical character than the idle wonders and conjectures of the rest of the crowd. The spire was entirely covered with sheets of gilded copper, and presented a surface to the eye as smooth as if it had been one mass of burnished gold. But Telouchkine knew that it was not one mass of anything; that the sheets of copper were not even uniformly closed upon each other; and above all, that there were large nails used to fasten them, which projected from the sides of the spire.

Having meditated upon these circumstances till his mind was made up, the mujik went to the government, and offered to repair the angel, without scaffolding, and without assistance, on condition of being reasonably paid for the time expended in the labour. The offer was accepted; for it was made in Russia, and by a Russian.

On the day fixed for the adventure, Telouchkine, provided with nothing more than a coil of cords, ascended the spire in the interior to the last window. Here he looked down at the concourse of people below, and up at the glittering "needle," as it is called, tapering far away above his head. But his heart did not fail him, and stepping gravely out upon the ledge of the window, he set about his task.

He cut a portion of the cord in the form of two long stirrups, with a loop at each end. The upper loops he fastened upon two of the projecting nails above his head, and placed his feet in the others. Then, digging the fingers of one hand into the interstices of the sheets of copper, he raised up one of his stirrups with the other hand, so as to make it catch a nail higher up. The same operation he performed on behalf of the other leg, and so on alternately. And thus he climbed, nail by nail, step by step, stirrup by stirrup, till his starting-post was undistinguishable from the golden surface, and the spire had dwindled, and dwindled, and dwindled in his embrace, till he could clasp it all round.

So far, so well. But he had now reached the ball—a globe of between nine and ten feet in circumference. The angel, the object of his visit, was *above* this ball, and even concealed from his view by its smooth, round, and glittering expanse. Only fancy the wretch at that moment, turning up his grave eyes, and graver beard, to an obstacle that seemed to defy the daring and ingenuity of man !

But Telouchkine was not dismayed. He was prepared for the difficulty ; and the means by which he essayed to surmount it exhibited the same *prodigious* simplicity as the rest of the feat.

Suspending himself in his stirrups, he girded the

needle with a cord, the ends of which he fastened round his waist; and so supported, he leaned gradually back till the soles of his feet were planted against the spire. In this position he threw, by a strong effort, a coil of cord over the ball; and so coolly and accurately was the aim taken, that at the first trial it fell in the required direction, and he saw the end hang down on the opposite side.

To draw himself up into his original position ; to fasten the cord firmly round the globe ; and with the assistance of this auxiliary to climb to the summit —were now an easy part of his task ; and in a few minutes more Telouchkine stood by the side of the angel, and listened to the shout that burst like sudden thunder from the concourse below, yet came to his ear only like a faint and hollow murmur.

The cord, which he had now an opportunity of fastening properly, enabled him to descend with comparative facility; and the next day he carried up with him a ladder of ropes, by means of which he found it easy to effect the necessary repairs.

Drawn by A.G. Vickers.

Engraved by R. Wallis.

The Birinskie and part of the Fortress

From the Neva. St Petersburg.

London, Published Oct.ʳ 1, 1835, for the Proprietor by Longman & Cᵒ Paternoster Row. Bonner & Cᵒ Paris. Asher Berlin.

Printed by India

CHAPTER VIII.

INSTEAD of returning directly across the river
from the fortress—a corner of which presents itself
in the opposite view—the reader is requested to
proceed by water to the Exchange, that columned
building in front.

The façade is formed by a vast and beautiful
Doric colonnade, surmounted by a suitable entablature; but this is encumbered and crushed by what

looks like the roof and part of the wall of an enormous house. The interior, however, is grand and imposing. A rostral column at each side near the river, from which the edifice retires a little way, is to my taste a grievous deformity.

Near the Exchange, proceeding along the quay, is the Academy of Sciences, founded in 1720 by Peter the Great; with a Museum which must be considered still in its infancy, and even with this apology is by no means worthy of the country. A cast of Peter's own face, taken after death, is perhaps one of the best things in it. The severe sagacity of expression of this wonderful savage, seems to have been tamed and softened by the touch of a still grimmer king than he, and the change gives more of human interest. There is besides a portrait, by "an out-of-doors artist"—the sign-board of a public house in Tower Street, London, where Peter went sometimes to drink on his way to work. The landlord, whose name was Edward Wild, on discovering the rank of his guest, hung up his portrait at the door, and re-baptized his house "The Czar of Muscovy." I believe it was the Emperor Alexander who devoutly transferred the relic to St. Petersburg.

A huge elephant, brought to the Tsar in 1713 by the Persian ambassador, is seen here stuffed, and in good preservation. When coming through Astrakan, the astonished people fell down before this undreamed-of monster, and worshipped him as a god; but soon after arriving in Russia his mortal

nature was sufficiently proved by his falling a victim
to the climate. The mammoth standing near him,
in the skeleton, did not prove to be so enormous an
animal as I was prepared to expect. It must be
recollected, however, that he wants the thickness of
the muscle, flesh, fat, and skin enjoyed by his
neighbour. Perhaps it is needless to say, that he
is not quite a genuine mammoth. Many of the
parts are manufactured from analogy with the
others: but still, from the numerous specimens
both here and at Moscow, it is impossible to doubt
that a great portion is now found of this creature,
who has vanished away, leaving only his bones for
a monument to tell that he once lived, and moved,
and had his being upon the earth. After the
elephant and mammoth may be mentioned the giant
of Peter the Great, who, like the former animal, is
stuffed in his skin.   This hideous and horrible
object is now stowed away in a dimly-lighted cellar,
where only such prying persons as myself are likely
to find him.

One of the objects, and the first, I believe, which
was presented to the institution, is the branch of a
tree in the form of a bow with the cord and arc
distinct. This, however, is common in the forests
of Russia. I have myself repeatedly seen pines
with but one stem for several feet from the ground,
then separating into two for many feet more, and
then uniting again, and forming one tall majestic
tree. One might imagine that there were two vege-
table lives in a single body, striving to separate, and

for a time effecting their deliverance, yet eventually
compelled by an irresistible fate to re-unite. Occasionally, however, the efforts of imprisoned nature
are more successful. The two particles of life
shoot up in one trunk till they have gained a
certain degree of strength, and then slowly and
gradually diverge into distinct trees. I wished
much to see the stem of one of these double trees
when sawed near the ground, but never had an
opportunity.

The Academy of Arts — to which I had the
advantage of being conducted by M. Sincofski the
well known journalist—is at some distance farther
on, and is generally reported by connoisseurs to be
the most perfect building in this city. With sub-
mission, however, I think that the Doric portico in
the centre is not in proportion with the rest of the
edifice. Had the curved line which it forms been
produced in its whole length horizontally, this
discrepancy would not have existed; but as it is,
unless the spectator stands very near, his eye cannot
make allowance for the real magnitude of the portico, and thus the effect of the whole is injured.
Let any one stand on the opposite bank of the river,
which is the proper point of view, and this circumstance cannot fail to strike him.

The only remarkable work of art I observed in
the place, and perhaps the only remarkable specimen
of Russian art in existence, was Bruloff's famous
picture of the Last Days of Pompeii. It is easier to
abuse a piece of this kind than to criticise it. It

belongs to the romantic school of art; and the conventional language of connoisseurship only applies to the classic, for and by which it was formed. There is nothing like this picture in existence. It stands alone for good and bad; and the conception is not more remarkable in both ways than the execution.

The foreground is illumined by lightning, and the back ground by fire; but you see the one through the other, and both become more ghastly by the union. The technical objections to this mode of lighting the scene I do not understand, as I am not a connoisseur; but it struck me that it was not sufficiently evident how and whence came the preternatural glare shed over the figures. There are three groups of these that seem to stand out of the canvass. On the left a man and a woman crouching, as they fly, under a cloak to preserve them from the burning, withering shower; in the middle a dead mother, and her beautiful child looking round in innocent consternation; and towards the right a man and a boy piously engaged in carrying an old man away with them from the fatal spot.

The limbs of the last group present the most extraordinary specimen I ever saw of the effects which may be produced by colours alone, without the aid of artificial light. Even when within a very few feet from the picture you can hardly persuade yourself that it is a plain surface, or that you cannot "catch the strong fellow by the leg." This most daring and original work is in many places

M

slovenly and unfinished; but with all its faults—
and their name is legion—it bears the stamp of
genius, and the connoisseurs may say what they
will.

Between the Academy of Sciences and that of
Arts, the Isaak's bridge leads across the river to
that grand centrical square, round which I have
been hovering so long. It is usually divided into
three squares, or places (plochchad in Russian),
that belonging to the palace, to the Admiralty, and
to the statue of Peter the Great; but as the whole
form a single oblong square, without any real
divisions, it is better for the sake of simplicity to
regard it as one—the heart of the city.

This immense oblong area runs parallel with the
river, which forms one of its sides; while the opposite side is bound in by the palace of the Etat
Major, the War Office, and the new Isaak's church.
The north-eastern angle is closed by a canal; and
the north-western by the palace of the Senate, and
that of the Holy Synod. Within the area, and
built upon the river side, stand the Admiralty, the
Winter Palace, and the Hermitage; the first of
these buildings occupying the greater part of the
entire length.

On landing from the Isaak's bridge—and the
word landing is well applied, since it is a bridge of
boats—the monument of Peter the Great arrests
the attention; and the visitor, on entering the finest
quarter of St. Petersburg, does homage to the
founder of the city.

Drawn by A. G. Vickers.

Engraved by T. Higham.

The Stone Bridge of the Admiralty,
St. Petersburg.

London, Published Oct. 1, 1835, for the Proprietor by Longman & Co. Paternoster Row, Bossange & Co. Paris, Asher Berlin.

Printed by Woodall & Clark

In the view annexed, the statue is seen on the left of the bridge, appearing in relief against the distant columns of the new and unfinished Isaak's church. Still farther to the left are the vast buildings of the Admiralty, which occupy the whole of the rest of the space. The monument of Peter, every body knows, derives a great portion of its reputation from the rock which serves as a pedestal for the equestrian figure. It is in the form of a precipice; and the horseman, who has just attained the summit, sits calmly and majestically on the saddle, while his steed is careering on its hind legs. Beneath, trampled under foot, is a huge serpent, which, being connected, although hardly perceptibly, with the flowing tail of the animal, assists in maintaining the equilibrium of the statue.

The rock was found near the village of Lachta in Carelia, eleven versts distant from St. Petersburg. It lay, huge and solitary, in a morass on the Gulf of Finland. No other stone was near, nothing which could account for its presence, or claim geological kindred with its substance. It was a curiosity and a wonder in itself; and looked as if it had been turned out of the hands of nature, expressly for the monument of a giant. It was chiefly formed of granite; but contained besides crystals, agates, topazes, cornelians, amethysts, &c. &c.—in short it was a miracle. No vestiges of these riches, it must be owned are now to be seen—at least thay are not discernible from the rails which surround the monument; but in corroboration, I may mention that Mr. W. Richardson, who travelled there in 1784, informs us that onyx earrings, sleeve-buttons, &c. were made from the fragments of this stone, and were very beautiful from the high polish they took.

The original dimensions were forty-two feet long, twenty-one high, and thirty-four broad. These I receive from Tooke, since he is invested with historical dignity; but travellers are not agreed in this case any more than others, even in matters of fact. A road was made from the spot where the colossus lay to the water's edge; and then brass slips were inserted under the stone, which was to roll upon cannon balls in metal grooves. In this manner was a weight of between fourteen and fifteen hundred tons, conveyed to the Gulf, drawn by windlasses worked by five hundred men; and there it was embarked for St. Petersburg in *camels*, a species of vessel which will be hereafter described.

If the French artist Falconet had let this work of nature alone, simply placing his own on the summit, all would have been well. It was necessary, however, to cut, and to carve, and to polish, and to make so rude and savage a mass look pretty and polite. The consequence was that the stone was irreparably spoiled. Its size, in which consisted a great part of its grandeur, was much diminished; and the effect of this paltry and effeminate chisel has been, to give the rock the appearance of having been scooped and sliced with a knife. Nothing, of course, can restore the magnificence it has lost; but if somebody was to round the edges of these scoops and slices, on and beneath the summit, it would become less precise, and look like a cliff which had been worn away by the waves.

It is usually said that this pedestal is formed of a single block of stone. In reality, however, it is in three pieces; although the middle one contains the vast bulk of the mass. It is sufficiently evident that the fragment at what may be called the tail of the stone, formed originally a part of it, and was broken by accident; but the other, in front, an immense mass under the summit of the cliff, appears to me to exhibit a considerable difference in composition and even in colour.

With regard to the figures, I can only join in the eulogium bestowed by other travellers. The metal of which they are formed is principally copper, with some tin and zinc, and the weight of the whole is forty-four thousand and forty-one pounds, not including ten thousand pound weight of iron inserted in the hinder part of the horse to preserve the equipoise. The figure of the Emperor is eleven feet high, and that of the horse seventeen feet The cost of the whole work amounted to eighty-five thousand pounds.

On one side of the space in which the monument stands, are the palaces of the Senate and Synod; and on the other, the south-western wing of the Admiralty. The two former buildings are chiefly distinguished for those Brobdignagian dimensions which in general characterize the public offices of this colossal empire. In the conference-hall of the Senate there are preserved in a silver shrine the laws of Catharine II., said to be in her own handwriting.

The Admiralty is not only the largest but perhaps the finest building in St. Petersburg. The immense length of the principal façade, however, rather injures the effect than otherwise; and, in fact, it might serve to form three distinct façades, one in the middle, and one at each end. The middle is neither so simple, nor to my taste, so beautiful as the others; but it is massive and imposing, and even the colossal statue at each side of the gate, bearing the celestial and terrestrial globes, are not out of keeping. Above the gate is a massive Doric entablature; from which rises the tower, surrounded by a gallery supported by Ionic columns, and surmounted by a dome, cupola, and spire, the three last covered with plates of fine gold.

The façade at either end (still to consider them distinct) is separated from the centre one by a range of buildings only one story high, with attic, and of immense length. They consist of a Doric portico for the centre-piece, with a pediment ornamented at each angle with a statue, and on either side a Doric colonnade. The whole is chaste and elegant; but perhaps the pediment is a little more charged which sculpture than suits the graceful simplicity of the order to which it belongs. This, however, is a fault so common, even in buildings of the highest rank, as scarcely to be considered one at all. The pediment seems naturally to belong to the sculptor as a field for the exercise of his art, without reference to the building of which it is a component part. The Admiralty was formerly defended by a ditch and ramparts, but instead of these, there is now a promenade, planted with small trees, and called the Boulevards.

When Peter the First determined to make St. Petersburg a great naval station, he seemed to treat with equal contempt the obstacles interposed by nature and by man; and his successors, either from pious respect to his memory, or from royal obstinacy, adhere to this day to his plans. Ships of the line are still built at the Admiralty—which a vessel drawing nine feet of water can neither approach nor leave! A late writer says *seventeen* feet, which is perhaps a mistake of the press.

When the ship is built, the question is how to get her down the river; and the task is always difficult and expensive, although performed with great ingenuity. A vessel is brought to the building-yard, called a *camel*, and which may be described as a huge hollow box. It is then filled with water, and sunk so far that on its sides being opened its enormous cargo may be floated into it. The box, which contains the entire bottom of the ship, is then screwed up, and pumped. As the water goes out the machine rises; till at length it floats so high as to be able to get over the bar, and deliver this strange passenger in triumph to the Gulf of Finland.

After traversing the line formed by the façade of the Admiralty, and which would of itself form a very tolerable forenoon's walk for a lady, the Winter Palace presents itself—opposite the north-east side of the former edifice. This imperial abode may be called antique for St. Petersburg, having been built by the Empress Elizabeth; and it is remarkable for its size, its dingy colour, and its bad taste. It consists of two stories above the vaults, ornamented with columns nearer the Composite than any other order; the *upper* resting on a huge square block of stone, and the lower with scarcely any base at all.

The interior of this palace is truly worthy of a monarch. It has been fully described, however, by a writer who is fond of kings and courts, and in whose eyes emperors and empresses, and all things pertaining thereto, are something more than earthly. I question whether there is any prince in Europe better lodged than the Emperor of Russia—and certainly no one can have a finer crown. Such a blaze of brilliants I never saw before! The imperial chapel, although a little gaudy, is exquisitely beautiful.

Every thing here worth seeing—and that is to say the whole house—was pointed out to my attention by General S——, whose kindness was unremitting during the whole of my visit to Russia, and whose influence I afterwards felt sensibly in my reception even at Moscow. If in the course of my tour, I say any thing—and I fear I shall say very many things—to shock his noble enthusiasm in favour of his country and his Emperor, I trust he will try to pardon me.

The Hermitage, the favourite haunt of Catharine II. when she wished to retire to as much solitude as an Empress surrounded by a brilliant court could desire, is connected with the Winter Palace by a covered gallery. It is now chiefly remarkable as being the repository of a museum of paintings, greater, I should think, in the numerical meaning of the word, than that of the Louvre and Luxembourg put together. I entered, with the intention of taking rough notes of the more remarkable works of art, or rather of the impression they produced upon me; but I speedily found that more days than I could afford hours would have been requisite for such a task. The counterfeits are said to be numerous; and in so vast a collection this must necessarily be the case.

The first thing that struck me was a work of Ruysdael, which is either the original, or one of several copies. It consists of a piece of water covered with weeds, and aquatic flowers floating on the surface. It is lighted through the trees behind, and so breathlessly still, that one is afraid to speak.

A Europa by Guido Reni drew my attention by its exquisite delicacy united with the most luxurious beauty. The complexion is inimitable.

A young lady playing the piano, by Carlo Dolce. She is drawn in satin, sparkling with gold, and while touching the keys, without consciousness of

music, is turning round a most lovely face to notice
the effect produced by her charms upon the company.   This young lady, by the halo round her head,
I discovered to be Saint Cecilia.

I could not admire the Rafaelles, whether
genuine or not, although I thought it my duty to
try; but a small picture hanging near, with the
name of Solario, gave me infinite pleasure.   A
young mother is suckling her child, and gazing upon
its face with a truly radiant joy; while the babe in
an extacy of pleasure is twisting up its limbs, and
pulling lustily one of its little great toes.

The Corregios appeared to me to be very indifferent.   There were plenty of Teniers; but those I
am not connoisseur enough to admire.   The care
with which every uncouth figure is finished may be
very praiseworthy, but it does not make the figures
pleasing.

Surrounded by the cocks and hens of Winart,
there was the exquisite Kuyp, or else a copy just
as good.   A group of cattle, standing in a hazy
sun-set beside a sleeping sea: such are the simple
materials of this delightful picture.

There were numberless Rembrandts, and some
very fine.   For my part, I looked longest at a Virgin and Child, watched by angels—all natives of
Holland; the holy mother with her feet upon a
chauffe-pied, and various tools hanging against the
wall to show that her husband was a carpenter.
This differs from the Russian tradition of the Virgin, which is more poetical, if not more scriptural.

According to this account, Mary was a servant of the Jewish temple, and being a child, was admitted behind the sanctum. She grew up in the beauty of holiness, till, having attained the age of fifteen, this became no longer proper; and it was decided by the aged priests, who had come to love her as their own daughter, and who dreaded the idea of parting with her, that one of them should make her his wife. The lot, accordingly, fell upon Joseph, who was then eighty years of age.

The French gallery has many good pictures. There is one of Vernet, which struck me as being the best I have seen of the artist. It is, as usual, a water-piece. The moon is shining on the sea, and her silvery light is beautifully, and not extravagantly contrasted with that of a fire kindled on the beach, and of a torch at the prow of a fishing-boat.

The Russian gallery is small and meagre.

The Spanish, on the contrary, is highly interesting; although the warm glare of almost all the pictures, which seems the livery of the Spanish school, gives a sameness to the aspect of the room. I had before only known, or only recollected, Murillo as the painter of low Spanish life; but here are several pieces of another cast, particularly the Nativity, and the Repose in Egypt. The latter is astonishingly lovely; and the Virgin, is, indeed, without exception, the most beautiful of the very few beautiful Virgins I have seen. The colouring is admirable, although warm and rich to excess.

I was struck also with a female figure by Gaspar

Becerra. The face possesses infinite beauty; and the large dark eyes beam with an expression almost too voluptuous.

Of the English school, there is *one* specimen. The piece,—which could not have made a strong impression upon me, since I already forget what it was,—is inscribed "Thomas Jones." It was painted for the Empress Catharine, and engraved also by her order. There is likewise in the same collection, but not exhibited to the public, a picture painted for her majesty by Sir Joshua Reynolds. The subject—the infant Hercules strangling the serpent—involved an allegory which the empress perhaps did not wish to flaunt in the eyes of the world. The infant Hercules, some people might have interpreted infant Russia, while every tyro knows that the serpent is the type of the universe.

In the dining-room of this Hermitage of the voluptuous Catharine, no servants attended; the dishes rising on small tables through trap doors. When a person wished to change his plate, he placed a paper upon it, inscribed with what he wanted, and striking it on the middle, it immediately disappeared, and almost as immediately another re-appeared with what was demanded. At other signals, every thing vanished, and a new course made its appearance. The amusements here were derived from the fine arts, &c.—books, paintings, statues, curiosities, models of inventions, gems, music, billiards, cards, and winter and summer gardens. In the winter gardens, as at present, the

fruits and flowers of the south were gathered in the
dead of the year ; and the birds which lived in this
perpetual summer were prevented from escaping
into winter by minute wirework.

The rules by which she governed the society
admitted into her paradise, are hung up in a corner,
and covered with a small curtain. Captain Jones
gives the *original* of these rules, in French, and
translates it into English. The original, however, is in Russian, and his French is only a para-
phrase. The following translation was made for
me, as literally as possible, by Mr. J. C——, to
whom I am indebted for many more kindnesses.

Catharine, I may remark in passing, was still
more an enemy to ceremony at the palace of Tsar-
cocœlo; for there, any lady who rose up on the
empress entering or leaving a room was fined in a
silver ruble.

RULES,

*By which all who enter these doors must conduct
themselves.*

I.

To leave every kind of rank at the door, likewise hats, and above all, swords.

II.

Disputes about prerogative, pride, and such like,
should any exist, to be left at the door.

N

III.

To be lively; but not to spoil, nor to break, nor to bite any thing.

IV.

To sit, to stand, to walk about, as each thinks proper, without regard to other people.

V.

To speak with moderation, and not too loud, that the ears and heads of the rest may not ache.

VI.

To dispute without warmth or passion.

VII.

Not to sigh, nor to yawn; and so entail tedium and heaviness on the rest.

VIII.

Any innocent game that one may project not to be found fault with by the others.

IX.

To eat of the sweet and the savoury, but to drink with moderation, that each may always find his feet on going out of the doors.

X.

All wrangling to end in the room; and what goes in at one ear should go out at the other before the party goes out of the door.

Should any one offend against the aforesaid on testimony of two witnesses, for every fault the offender must drink a glass of cold water, not excepting the ladies, and read aloud a page of the Telemachid.

And whoever offends against three clauses in one evening shall learn six lines of the Telemachid by heart.

And if any one offend against the ten, he must be no more admitted.

Opposite the Winter Palace, and midway between this edifice and the palace of the Etat Major, where the military business of the empire is transacted, stands the monument commonly called the Alexandrine Column, from its having been erected to the memory of the late emperor.

This object has a truly noble and majestic appearance from whichever point of view it is beheld. The shaft is formed of a single block of marble brought from the quarries of Finland, and, exclusively of pedestal and capital, is eighty-four feet high. The pedestal is of granite, with allegorical bas-reliefs in bronze; and on the summit stands an angel, holding a cross with the left hand, and pointing to heaven with the right. The inscription, on the side of the pedestal next the palace, is nearly as simple as that of the monument of Peter the Great. It contains merely these words: To Alexander I. grateful Russia.

On the eleventh of September, 1834, the conse-

cration of this column took place; which Mr.
Vickers, with his usual power, describes to the eye
of the reader in the next page. The day before,
much anxiety and uncertainty had prevailed in St.
Petersburg; for it seemed as if Heaven itself was
about to interpose. The beautiful, but terrible
Neva, forced back by the waters of the Gulf of
Finland, had risen upon her granite quays, and
threatened once again to devour the city which so
often before had been the victim of her wrath.
The alarm-cannon were fired; and the population,
already looking forward with intense longing for the
scene of to-morrow, were thrown into dismay.

The Neva, however, was more placable than on
former occasions; her swoln waters retired majestically; and that important morrow dawned upon
the metropolis in peace.

If the reader will only remember the description
which I have attempted to give of the grand square
where the ceremony was to take place, he may form
some idea of the scene it presented. Estrades were
formed all round that immense area; and these, with
the boulevards of the Admiralty, were crowded with
spectators. The windows, in like manner, were
stuck full of human heads; and the flat roofs of the
houses swarmed with their inhabitants. But in the
middle space, from side to side, from end to end,
nothing was to be seen but the glitter of arms and
the waving of military plumes.

At ten o'clock, the troops assembled at their
quarters; and, at eleven, on a signal from the guns

Drawn by A. G. Vickers.

Engraved by H. Jordan.

The Column of Alexander.

St. Petersburg.

London, Published Oct. 1, 1835, for the Proprietors, by Longman &C. Paternoster Row; Rittner & C.º Paris; Asher Berlin.

Printed by Fenner Sears

of the light artillery, already planted at the corner of the boulevards, they all debouched at one moment by the several issues appointed, and drew up in the square. This imposing mass was formed of eighty-six battalions of infantry, and one hundred and six and a half squadrons of cavalry, with two hundred and forty-eight pieces of artillery. All these various bodies were drawn up, facing the Alexandrine column, the pedestal of which was concealed from their view by flags.

The Emperor, who had attended divine service at the monastery of Saint Alexander Nevskoi, soon appeared upon the scene, with the Heir of the crown, and the Grand Duke Michael, and surrounded by a brilliant staff. All eyes were then turned towards a large verandah, in the form of a tent, at the window of the palace above the great gate, directly opposite the column, and provided with a flight of stairs descending to the street. There already stood the high civil functionaries, the members of the diplomatic body, the marshals of the nobility, and the deputies of commerce; and, precisely at noon, the high clergy were seen filing into it in procession, from the grand chapel of the palace, with their crosses and banners displayed, and followed by the Empress and the whole court. The business of the day then commenced.

The moment the procession appeared, the Emperor gave the word of command; and the whole array of troops presented arms like one man. The priests then thundered forth the Te Deum; and

emperor, empress, court, soldiers, spectators—
every living soul in that mighty concourse of human
beings—sunk upon their knees.

After the hymn, and a prayer for the imperial
family, the archdeacon recited prayers for the soul
of the Emperor Alexander; and, as he pronounced
the last words, the flags which had hitherto concealed the pedestal of the column fell, and disclosed
the monument. At this sight the troops again presented arms; a tremendous hurra rose from every
lip; and a burst of military music shook the square,
almost drowned by the thunder of the artillery, and
the deep roar of the cannon of the fortress.

Prayers were then recited for the Russian
army; and, when these were concluded, the clergy,
followed by the Empress and her whole train,
descended from the balcony. They walked in
procession round the column, the metropolitan
sprinkling it with holy water. The troops then
defiled before it, and the ceremony was finished.

CHAPTER IX.

Progress of civilization in Russia—condition of the nobles till Peter the Great—domestic imprisonment of wives—brutal treatment of them—marriages—ugliness punishable with the whip—corresponding want of refinement in the women—drunkenness—painting—age of Catharine II.—affranchisement of the nobility by Peter III.—private Chancery of Nicolas—business habits of the Emperor—form of government—code of laws—administration of the laws.

MALTEBRUN says that Russia "lost only its beard" by the reforms of Peter I. This is nothing more than a French bon mot; but still, taking it as literally true, it was a great deal to lose at one blow. With their beards, however, the boïars parted with prejudices as bristly, and almost as numerous as the hairs they contained; and notwithstanding the bloody struggles in which they were so constantly engaged, they became, in a space

of time unparalleled in the annals of civilization—
what they now are.

It would be a curious study to trace the progress
of Russian civilization, and its history would be far
from difficult to write. The space of time is brief,
the materials few, and the testimony conclusive.

In the latter half of the seventeenth century, the
author of the "Relation des Trois Ambassades,"
informs us, that "most men treat their wives as a
necessary evil, regarding them with a proud and
stern eye, and even beating them often." Olearius
says that it was a prodigious civility for a man to
allow another to see his wife. When this favour
was to be accorded, the lady walked into the room
after dinner, splendidly dressed, and presented a
cup of distilled spirits to the guest, drinking off one
herself. On one occasion the traveller was even
invited to salute his hostess; but astonished at such
an offer from a Russian, and dreading, no doubt,
that some insidious plan lurked under it, he
endeavoured to excuse himself.

Dr. Samuel Collins, physician to the tsar about
1670, consoles his readers with the intelligence that
the custom of tying up wives by the hair of the
head, and flogging them "begins to be left off."
This, however, he accounts for by the prudence of
the parents, who make it a provision in the marriage
contract that their daughters are not to be whipped,
struck, kicked, &c. &c. Some disorders nevertheless still took place, even in such an improved state of
society. One man, indeed, "put upon his wife a

shirt dipped in ardent spirits, and burnt her to death." But let us hope that this was not a very common case. The man, however, if we are to believe the doctor, was not prosecuted, there being "no punishment in Russia for killing a wife or a slave." On the other hand if a lady made away with her tyrant, she was buried up to the neck in the earth, and so suffered to die.

When no provision was made in the contract, according to the same authority, they were accustomed "to discipline their wives very severely." At marriage the bridegroom had a whip in one boot, and a jewel in the other, and the poor girl tried her fortune by choosing. "If she happen upon the jewel," says Collins, "she is lucky; if on the whip, she gets a lash." The bridegroom rarely saw his companion's face till after the knot was tied; but if he absolutely insisted upon this privilege, it was sometimes contrived that the lady passed through a street where he was stationed at a window. "If she be ugly, she pays for it soundly, may be the first time he sees her."

The women, it may be presumed, did not grow up into especial refinement under such discipline. Drunkenness was esteemed a very lady-like vice, if indeed, it was considered to be a vice at all. The day after a lady was at an entertainment, the hostess was accustomed to send to ask how she got home; and the prescriptive reply was this: "Her hospitality made me so tipsy that, indeed, I do not know how I got home!" I may add that Tooke, whose heroine is Catharine II., declares that "for a lady to be drunk was no reproach;" and we all know what sort of scenes took place at the court of Elizabeth.

It may be supposed that women, in whom ugliness was criminal, and punishable with the whip, were at great pains to disguise it. They painted to such excess that the beauty of their teeth, according to Collins, was completely destroyed; and hence came the custom of staining their teeth black. In the time of Olearius it was usual for the bridegroom to send a present of paint to his bride. This traveller, in 1636, saw the Grand Duchess and her ladies on horseback, astride, and "most wickedly bepainted."

What will no doubt be considered, however, as the very climax of barbarity, is a fact recorded by Tooke: that the women did not begin to wear stays till the commencement of the present century!

With regard to the men, their character up to a very late period, is treated with still less ceremony, if that be possible, by all travellers. According to them, they were the most ignorant and barbarous people in the world, destitute alike of moral principle and common decency. Even the representatives of the states assembled so pompously by Catharine—who died only in 1796—although composed no doubt of the first men of the various governments, went immediately on receiving the commemorative medal struck on the occasion, and sold it to the goldsmiths!

The rules of Catharine, given in the last chapter, sufficiently evidence the low state of politeness even at court; but with these it is necessary to take in conjunction the occupations and amusements of that very assembly, the objects of refinement by which they were surrounded, and the purer tastes which were thus engendered or gratified. If we do this, the whole picture will be found to represent the triumphant struggles of civilization in a contest which was no longer doubtful. But let us remember at the same time, that from the death of Peter the Great to that of Catharine II., there elapsed an interval of only seventy-one years; and that from the death of Catharine II. to the present moment, there is a space of only thirty-nine years. For Russia that united period stands in lieu of *nine centuries;* since it can be proved to a demonstration —if I have read historians and travellers aright— that Russia, before Peter, was not farther advanced in civilization than the rest of Europe in what is called the iron age.

The nobility were not affranchised till 1761 by Peter III. They were then permitted to wear arms or not as they chose, and to travel abroad. Catharine, his successor, allowed this ordinance to subsist, because as the nobles were obliged in etiquette to ask leave before setting out, she might (and did) refuse it when she chose. The same state of things remains at the present day. Leave is asked, and granted or not, as circumstances may determine. I was told that above eighty families or individuals of respectability had petitioned for the boon last year, and that about half the number had obtained it. The Russian nobility live well enough at home, but generally speaking, they have no money to spend abroad. If the restriction were withdrawn, there would in my opinion be fewer applications. No man now thinks of wearing a sword except when on military duty; but if an oukaz were issued prohibiting men from doing so without having asked and obtained permission, petitions would shower in from half the nobles in the empire.

The base and cowardly conspiracy against the life of the present emperor has retarded a good deal the progress of public liberty among the nobles; although, as I shall explain in a future chapter, it has been proportionably beneficial to those myriads of peasants who will one day be called the PEOPLE. The severity of the above restrictions on travelling (now only beginning to be relaxed), and that of the censorship on books, are part of the punishment inflicted on the nobles for the misconduct of a few. This, considering the relative condition of the two countries, and the important nature of the Russian conspiracy, is not nearly so harsh as the laws now promulgating against the liberty of the press in France, on pretext of the attempt of a single mean and companionless scoundrel.

In no other country, however, on the face of the earth, would a conspiracy of such a nature have been so leniently punished throughout On the occasion of the revolt of the strelitses, Peter the Great, besides causing many hundred other executions, cut off eleven heads with his own hand! The same difference is observable in the new institutions of Russia as compared with the older—and one of these institutions is so remarkable in itself, and so peculiar to the country, that this brief notice of the progress of civilization would be incomplete without it.

A Private Chancery existed in Russia from an early period, and must exist under every absolute government; but the one more especially known to history was erected, as some writers say, by Alexis the father of Peter the Great, although an imperial oukaz of Catharine II. attributes it to the latter. The crimes brought under the cognizance of this horrible tribunal, which is well described by Tooke in his life of Catharine, were at first attempts against the life of the emperor, against religion, and against the state: but all criminal cases came at length to be comprehended. The process began with the imprisonment, and occasionally with the execution of the accused. When the accuser failed in proof he was knouted three several times. His declaration was then received. The accused might in like manner suffer the knout instead of pleading, an occurrence which of course often took place, since it must have been impossible to prove his innocence of crimes alleged so mysteriously. If the judge was not convinced by either party, they were both knouted again; and then their guilt or innocence came to be determined by the constancy with which they suffered the flesh to be torn from their backs.

Station, age, and sex—all were alike unspared and undistinguished. The slightest accusation was listened to. To "cry the word" meant to denounce; and at this sound *"the word !"* uttered in a crowd, all fled as if from the plague. If "the word" was spoken by a servant against his master, the latter, even if the first lord in the land, was obliged to hasten to the next guard-house, and demand that they should both be sent to prison together.

This flourished under the reign of the *clement* Elizabeth, as she is usually called, on account of her having made a vow never to punish with death. Even an inferior magistrate was permitted to torture an accused by dislocating his shoulders, and tongues were cut out, and their owners banished to Siberia on the slightest whisper. People were taken from their beds, without trial, and thrust into a dungeon,—sometimes a subterranean one,—frequently for life. The clement Empress, who reigned from 1741 to 1761, shut up, it is supposed, in this private manner, upwards of 20,000 of her subjects. Peter III. recalled 17,000 of her exiles ; but of those of the Empress Anne, her predecessor, supposed to be equally numerous, three-fourths were never heard of more.

When the last-mentioned prince, the affranchiser, as we have seen, of the nobles, went one day to the senate, and found nobody there to attend to the business of the country, he sent for the senators, and reproved them sharply. His grandfather, Peter the Great, had already done more: he caned each of them soundly. Nicolas, the present emperor, took them by surprise in like manner; and, finding that neither words nor blows had been of any use, he organized, like Peter or Alexis, a Secret Chancery.

This is the plan by which the Emperor corrects the evils of the form of government, or rather, of the abuses inseparable from it. In Russia, it is not the people who are rebels against the constitution, but the emperor. He is engaged in a perpetual struggle against tyranny and misrule. The very comprehensive plan adverted to, is not a part of the administration of the laws, but a part of his own business as an individual; and the institution is called, "the Private Chancery of his majesty the Emperor."

It is divided into four branches; one watching over the great offices of the state, such as the senate, another over the courts of law, a third, over the police, and the fourth, over the charitable institutions. Through these different channels, complaints and abuses reach the ear of his majesty instantaneously. He is acquainted with the official conduct of each of his ministers; he is even aware of the regularity or irregularity of the attendance of the senators. It is needless to say, that the inquiries instituted there take place, not in form of law, but according to equity; they, in fact, answer the purpose of the nightly prowlings of the caliph Haroun Alraschid and his grand vizier.

But Nicolas is not a man who would refuse to perform these nightly prowlings in his own person, were they practicable through his vast empire. I felt intense curiosity with regard to the real character and conduct of an individual placed in so awfully responsible a situation; and, unless all Russia conspired to deceive me, I think I have been able to form some tolerably correct ideas on the subject.

No fatigue is too harassing for this " Barbarian," par excellence, of the north; no object is too great to be grasped by his vision, or too small to escape it. The gravest fraud in a report, and the minutest error in its grammar, are alike detected by the imperial censor; and this is the more startling to the reporter, as his delinquency, either in honesty or elegant composition, is in general brought home to him the very next day.

To effect this, Nicolas condemns each day to bear its own burthen. After coming home, perhaps from the theatre, he sits down to work; and he never thinks of going to bed till all is finished, if he should sit up till four o'clock in the morning. With regard to his character as a man of business, I heard only one dissentient voice in Russia: I was told by one of the officers of government, that he was beginning to relax in this extraordinary assiduity. I hope, and believe, that the information was untrue.

The proceedings of the Chancery are necessarily secret; it is, in short, a system of espionage, precisely similar in effect to that of Haroun Alraschid. In England, every thing is carried on in broad

day-light, except what is contrary to the laws;
but, in the country I am describing, peopled by a
fifteenth part of the human race, the great majority
of whom are still in the darkest ignorance, this is
manifestly impossible. The Chancery is, beyond a
doubt, the best thing in the Russian government;
and this form of government is the only one which
could hold the empire together for six months.

The form of government is *absolute*. There are,
no doubt, certain historical forms, usages, and tradi-
tions, which may be called the constitution of
Russia by those who are fond of names, because it
would be unsafe for the emperor to depart from
them. But, in reality, the constitution of Russia
is the will of the sovereign for the time being; and,
till the great mass of the people are awakened from
the profound ignorance in which they are at present
buried, it is well it is so. I cannot conceive what
the nation would gain by having for its rulers a
junta of kings, instead of a single autocrator. The
mistake usually fallen into on this subject, is to
imagine that the hundreds of thousands constitute
the people, and not the millions! At present, the
imperial will has no lawful check whatever; although the actions of the emperor are modified by
fear of the nobles on one hand, and fear of the mass
on the other. These two species of fear, as society
is constituted, both work in favour of the multitude.

It was the desire of Peter the Great, and of
almost all his successors, to collect the laws of the
empire; and various commissions were established

from time to time for the purpose. The difficulties, however, appear to have been found insurmountable, till his present majesty and his Private Chancery came into the field. I cannot look upon it as an achievement effected by any thing else than the business habits of the Emperor. The following is a (translated) extract from his manifesto published on the completion of the undertaking two years ago.

"Having recognized on our accession to the throne, the indispensable necessity of introducing into the whole body of the laws of our country a clear and systematic order, we commanded in an especial manner that they should be collected, and the collection published entire; and we further announced our will that there should afterwards be taken out from the mass, for the purpose of forming a body of uniform and regular laws, all such laws as are now in force in our empire, without changing in the slightest degree their spirit—the whole to be strictly pursued on the basis laid down in the year 1700 by Peter the Great.

"The execution of the first part of this plan was finished in 1830.

"With the aid of the Almighty, and after seven years assiduous labour, carried on under our personal direction, the accomplishment of the second part is now terminated. From the code of 1649 till the first of January, 1832, all the laws promulgated within that period of one hundred and eighty-three years, which have preserved through the changes of time even till our days their force and tenor, have been collected and classified according to their nature, only leaving out such clauses as have been repealed by subsequent laws; and with the exception of the regulations of the army by land and sea, and some others hereafter mentioned, all these laws have been arranged in a uniform system, divided into codes according to the principal distinctions of administrative and judiciary affairs. All the laws which have been promulgated *after* the 1st of January, 1832, or which may be so promulgated in the ordinary march of legislation, will be added every year in a supplement to the Body of Laws, according to the order of the above codes, and with reference to the proper article: so that the general system of laws being once established, it will preserve for ever its uniformity and identity.

" The most pressing and essential wants in the empire—justice and order in the administration— demand imperiously this measure. It guarantees the force and the action of the laws for the present, and establishes a solid basis for their gradual perfectibility in the future. It fulfils, in fine, the wishes by which our ancestors have been animated for a period, hardly interrupted, of one hundred and twenty-six years."

The next thing to be done, is to reform the administration of the laws—or, rather, to create it. This is at present the worst feature in the government of Russia. It is more allied to the ignorance and corruption of the East than to European civilization. If in England we are cursed with an overflow of lawyers, in what state must that country be in which any man whatever, educated or uneducated, may practise as a lawyer! A writer states, that, in 1826, there were two millions, eight hundred and fifty thousand cases came on before the tribunals of the empire. If this was true, one out of every five adult males must have been at law; but, even allowing it to be a mighty exaggeration, the evil must be enormous. The Emperor, by the great work already alluded to, has virtually given a code of laws to the country. An equally noble, and still more difficult task remains—that of providing for their being carried into execution by fixed and intelligible rules,—unalterable except by the imperial prerogative of mercy.

CHAPTER X.

Present state of society in St. Petersburg—dress—introduction of the national costume at court—low condition of literary society—inutility of learning the language—censorship of the press—books of luxury—novels—theatre and dramatic authors—police—movement of the population—classification—strange discrepancy in the numbers of the two sexes—births and deaths—marriages and suicides—climate—parting glance.

I have described St. Petersburg as being a city of the Russian nobles; and yet there the traveller will find no true specimen of Russian society. The natives are so completely intermingled with foreigners that it is hardly possible to tell which is which; and French being the language of all, you may fancy yourself at Paris.

At the time of the Swedish ambassador, whose travels are immortalized by Olearius, there was *one*

Russian lord who had laid aside the national costume; and the fact was thought so extraordinary that the name of this individual has been preserved by the journalist. At present, there is no man to be found among them so hardy as even to allow his clothes to be *made* by his own countrymen. There is, in fact, throughout this class of society a sickly craving after every thing foreign, and an unmanly affectation of scorn for every thing native. Little did Peter the Great think that his wise, and at that time necessary, plans should lead eventually to so much folly and bad taste.

In this state of things it is quite unnecessary to say, that the ladies, so far as dress is concerned, have metamorphosed themselves into Frenchwomen; but here a stand has been made, although somewhat late, by the genius of the country. I do not know whether it is the Emperor or Empress who deserves the credit of the new regulation; but since the first of January 1834, a modification of the national female costume has been introduced at court.

The Ladies of Honour wear a satin or velvet sarafan—a robe open before, and without sleeves—richly trimmed with gold. The sleeves of the underdress, a gown I presume it is called—or else a slip—reach to the wrist, where they are fastened by gold bracelets. The headdress consists of a richly ornamented crown, as it may be described, very nearly resembling in shape the one worn by the nurses; and from this hangs down behind, and partly over the shoulders, till it reaches the bend

of the knee, an immense white veil. No part of
the hair is seen except a little in front plainly
and smoothly braided on the brow.

The Maids of Honour wear also the national
sarafan, and a species of crown. The latter, however, does not encircle the head, but permits the
whole of the hair to be seen. This is plainly
braided in front like that of the others, but disposed
in a very large club behind ; to which is fastened a
thin veil, or scarf, which floats down the back.
Almost the whole of the arm is bare, the sleeves
being very short.

The love of foreigners, so prevalent here, is very
advantageous to the traveller. If decently introduced he may spend every evening in very agreeable
society ; and the oftener he frequents a particular
soirée the more welcome he finds himself. An
English gentleman has lately had the indiscretion to
publish a journal of his visits of this kind, giving his
opinion very frankly of individuals by name. On
one occasion he stigmatizes all the ladies at a
certain ball, the date and locale of which he
fixes with precision—all excepting some individuals
whom he mentions—as *ugly*. I would advise this
gentleman to choose any other country on the face
of the globe for his future wanderings. I can
assure him that even his " beautiful princesses " and
" charming ambassadresses " join in the indignation
of the ugly.

There can hardly be said to be such a thing as
literary society in St. Petersburg ; and, indeed, the

political interests and feelings of the few authors there are run to such an excess, as to place such a thing almost out of the question. The stranger, however, will not discover this at first. There is a frankness and heartiness about each individual, which, added to the genuine good-nature of the Russians, would make one imagine that "envy, hatred, malice, and all uncharitableness" could have no existence among them. Yet I have nowhere else met with such bitter dissensions. The love of literature *for itself* does not seem to me to exist in Russia.

I was desirous of including in this volume a catalogue raisonné of the Russian authors, and M. G——— volunteered to furnish it. He was prevented, no doubt, by his numerous and more important labours; but I am sorry he did not contrive to let me know in time, as he must have been aware that I had plenty of other means at command. The misery is, the necessity of being dependent upon native writers for any thing of the kind; but I need hardly say, that at present it is worth no man's while to study the Russian language.

I was one day conversing on this subject with M. M———, one of the secretaries of state, and head of the third section of the Chancery, when he made a very natural remark.

"It seems strange to me," said he, "that you English should travel in Russia for the avowed purpose of making yourselves acquainted with the manners and character of the people, yet without comprehending a single word of their language.

You come here with the grossest prejudices against us as a nation. You see every thing different from what you have been accustomed to at home, except the manners of some dozen families whom you visit. You make no inquiries, no reflections, no allowances. You examine this rude but mighty colossus through your opera glass, or from the windows of your travelling chariot. In the towns your valet de place is your prime authority ; in the country you wander about in utter darkness, unable to understand a single object, and unable to ask a single question. You then return home satisfied with having attained the object of your tour ; and sit down, without a single malevolent feeling in your breast, but out of pure ignorance, to add to the mass of falsehoods and absurdities with which Europe is already inundated !"

I could not help acknowledging the justice of these remarks ; but I told M. M——— that Russia would gradually become known notwithstanding our ignorance of her language; and in the meantime that he should not himself fall into the illiberality or inconsiderateness he condemned in others.

"The craving after knowledge," said I, "or after mere novelty, which exists in civilized Europe, sends forth every year innumerable travellers to all countries on the face of the globe. The traveller in France possesses a knowledge of the French language—in Italy, of the Italian—in Germany, of the German—because in all these countries there is such a constant action and re-action between the national

P

character and the national literature, that they cannot by possibility be studied separately. In Russia there is no national literature. The great mass of the people—I may say the NATION—is still in a state of profound ignorance; and no inducement exists to make any mere literary man undergo the life-long labour of acquiring a language which has even no affinity with the other European tongues. French is the language of the civilized classes in Russia; and I may add, by way of illustration, although without meaning to institute a comparison which in this case would be both unjust and absurd —that the traveller in Africa is thought to be sufficiently well qualified for the journey by a knowledge of Arabic."

The censorship already alluded to is no doubt a serious weight upon the literature of the country; and it seems to me to be the most inefficient, as well as the most odious of all the measures of arbitrary power. Against what class of society is this prohibition directed? The lower classes either cannot or do not read; and is there any officer of government so profoundly ignorant as not to know, that any individual of the upper classes may obtain with perfect facility any prohibited work whatever? For my part I read nothing but prohibited books all the time I was in Russia.

I cannot help thinking that the Emperor is ignorant of the ridiculous excess to which the censorship is carried. Even bygone matters of historical notoriety must be slurred over or distorted into falsehood. Murder must be called natural death; or the book shall appear to the public with a gap as wide and ominous as the gash of the assassin's knife. Who would not laugh to think that the light page which I am now writing— in spite of the comparatively favourable view of the country which a regard for truth and reason has compelled me to take—will be *cut out,* before the Picturesque Annual is allowed to circulate in Russia !

In general, books of the fine arts have less sale than might be expected from the wealth and voluptuousness of the nobles. Even one lately published in Russian, dedicated to a description of St. Petersburg, and embellished with engravings, has failed as a speculation. Judging from the portion which was already translated into French—and which I have found of great use in matters of detail—I would say that the " Panorama of St. Petersburg" is well worthy of public patronage. Its price, however,— a hundred rubles—will prevent it from ever becoming extensively popular.

Novel-writing, on the other hand, is a very flourishing trade. Known authors receive from six to eight hundred pounds for their copyright; and if unknown, the bookseller prints, and they take their chance of success.

The theatre is in the hands of government: one advantage of which is, that the actors, after twelve years' service may retire whenever they choose with a pension. I was told that first-rate artists were not invited to join the German company, lest it should prejudice the Russian. This, however, I disbelieve, from the circumstance that the pension of foreign actors is two thousand rubles, while that of natives is only one thousand. Surely no national partiality is exhibited here.

Dramatic authors usually give the first night of the piece for the benefit of a popular actor, which insures its being well played, and well received. They make from one to two hundred pounds at St. Petersburg; and, if successful, the drama is reproduced at Moscow on the same terms.

The only apparent police of this city are the pole-axe men. They are of use in directing the stranger to any house he may be in search of, as they are in general Fins, and know how to read. At night these men challenge the passers-by; who may answer, if English, "Hold your tongue!"—for Pole-axe always takes it for granted that "all's well." I heard a great deal about the system of police spies, but saw nothing of it either here or at Moscow. All the stories were at second-hand—I never happened to know any one who was incommoded personally. At the passport offices the people are perfectly polite. If the Chancery and the Police were a little nearer each other, the stranger would have nothing whatever to complain of; although I have heard that a good deal of trouble falls to the share of the hotel keepers.

The best hotel in the city is Mrs. Wilson's in the Galerna Oulitza, behind the English quay.

This is an establishment which every one must have pleasure in praising; for the traveller finds there not only all the comforts of an English inn, but many of the advantages of a private circle. The terms for board and lodging on the most liberal scale are eight rubles a day.

St. Petersburg is thirty-five versts in circumference, and from eight to nine long. The number of inhabitants, however, is far from being in proportion to so immense an area. The following table will show the movement of the population fron 1725 to 1832.

Year.	Reign.	Amount of Population.
1725	Peter the Great	75,000
1735	Anne	105,000
1750	Elizabeth	138,000
1765		162,000
1775		185,000
1785	Catharine II.	195,000
1795		208,000
1805		295,000
1820	Alexander	422,891
1825		433,112
1831	Nicolas	448,221
1832		449,368

This population of 449,368 souls is distributed as in the following table.

Clergy	2,188
Nobility	34,079
Soldiers	39,437
Merchants	10,833
Bourgeois	36,725
Inscribed in Corps de Métiers	27,279
Domestics	94,009
People of all trades	66,366
Peasants	127,867
Strangers	7,199
Inhabitants of the suburb of Okhta	3,386
	449,368

The distribution of the sexes, however, is the most extraordinary feature in this mass of population. In the above grand total there are 294,468 men and only 154,900 women !—a discrepancy which merits explanation.

Of the hundred and twenty-seven thousand peasants, there are from fifty to sixty thousand who reside only a part of the year in the city. These are the mujiks from the interior, who travel many hundred versts to seek employment for the spring and summer, leaving their wives at home to manage their little farms. The Hay Market, a view of which is annexed, is the best place to see these specimens of the genuine Russian. This is one cause of the deficiency in the female population.

Drawn by A.G. Vickers.

Engraved by W. Chevalier.

The Haymarket.
St. Petersburg.

London, Published Oct.r 1, 1835, for the Proprietor, by Longman & Co. Paternoster Row, Bruner & Co. Paris. Asher, Berlin.

Another is, that, of the remainder of the peasantry—the ninety-four thousand domestics—and the sixty-six thousand trades-people or artificers resident in the city, a very considerable number have left their families at a distance, and only visit them on a rare occasion. In addition to these causes, it may be mentioned that the high clergy are all unmarried, being monks, and that a very great proportion of the nobility are employés of the government, and others, who flock to the metropolis in quest of fortune before they think of looking out for a wife.

As for the great and steady increase of the population, this must be attributed, firstly, to the number of workmen, who, tired of their migrations, and perhaps deprived by death of the charm of that ark to which they were accustomed to return, sit down every year as residents in the city ; and, secondly, to the colonies of natives and foreigners attracted by the policy of the emperors to the capital. It is necessary to look for the increase in these causes alone ; for, startling as the fact may appear, the population does not increase of itself.

From 1770 to 1790, which is reckoned a *favourable* period, the difference between births and deaths was only 3630, while the increase in the number of inhabitants for the same period was 20,000. In the first ten years of the present century there were born 41,887 and 39,223 girls, while there died 68,082 males and 37,372 females, leaving on the side of mortality a balance of 25,344 individuals. In this period the population was increased by 65,000.

In 1832 the births were 10,167, and the deaths
15,197—a difference of 5,720 in one year.

From all this one would imagine the city to be
frightfully unhealthy; and even M. Bachoutsky, to
whom I am indebted for many details which a
stranger could not readily come at, seeks to explain
a part of the mystery by the suicidal stays, bands,
&c. of the women of quality. These women, however, form so trifling a portion of the population,
that if they were all to die together, the loss would
hardly be perceived by the statictician. The cause
must be sought for in the preceding paragraphs,
where it is clearly explained. The balance in favour
of mortality is owing to the vast numbers of males,
either resident or migratory, who, without having
added to the births, lay their bones every year in the
cemeteries of St. Petersburg.

To take, for example, the first ten years of the present century, in which there were born 39,223 girls
and 41,887 boys, we find the deaths 37,372 females
and *sixty-eight thousand* males. If you make the
number of male deaths correspond in the usual ratio
with that of the female deaths, you leave the natural
surplus in favour of the increase of human life.

The births here are as one to fifty-two of the
population; while in Paris they are as one to thirty-
one; but taking the above circumstances into account, the balance is in favour of St. Petersburg
rather than otherwise.

For the last few years the average number of
women compared with that of men is as forty-five

to a hundred; but unhappily the marriages do not take place even in proportion. From 1811 to 1821 the number was one to every 200 inhabitants; but this has gone on diminishing until it is now one to 340! Suicides bear a proportion of one to 20,360, which is pretty nearly the same as in Paris. In St. Petersburg, however, these crimes are usually committed in a paroxysm of passion; while in the French capital they take place upon reflection, and proceed from what young ladies call a philosophical despair.

The climate of St. Petersburg is delightful for a short time in summer. There is then no night. The soft glowing evening is met midway by the rich dawn; and at this season the Neva, with its green islands, is inexpressibly beautiful. Of the rest of the year, the reader may form some judgment from the following observations made by Count Sternberg during two hundred and thirty-two days.

In that period there were a hundred and nineteen days when it froze consecutively, and only twenty-five when it did not freeze at all. In a hundred and seventy-three the barometer stood *below* the freezing point. In sixty-nine it snowed, in a hundred and twelve it rained, in fifty-one there was fog, and in two hail.

The springs appear to be getting worse. On the nineteenth of May it was extremely cold, the ground covered with snow, and although by no means sensitive on such points, I was obliged to order my bed-room to be heated as in winter. The

inundations of the Neva in general take place
between the seventeenth of August and the twenty-
third of November—and they too appear to be
getting worse, as the following table of the rise of
the waters will show.

Years.	Feet.	Inches.	Years.	Feet.	Inches.
1721	7	4	1756	7	3
1723	7	7	1777	10	7
1726	8	2	1788	7	5
1729	7	1	1802	7	5
1744	7	0	1824	13	7
1752	8	5			

I have now given a hasty sketch of St. Petersburg,
or rather of its more prominent details, leaving
alone as much as possible the objects enlarged upon
by other travellers. The annexed view of the
Admiralty from the quay, by moonlight, will suffice
as a parting glance.

Drawn by A. G. Vickers.

Engraved by J. T. Willmore.

The Admiralty from the Palace Quay,
St Petersburg.

London. Published Oct.ʳ 1. 1835, for the Proprietor. by Longman & Cᵒ Paternoster Row, Rümer & Cᵒ Paris. Adler Berlin.

Printed by Mℯℐᵈℯ Ꙭ Pℯᵗᵗℯ

CHAPTER XI

Departure from St. Petersburg—the one thing needful to a traveller—inns and living—peasantry on the road—musical instruments—national songs—the Korovoda—curious remnant of paganism—dress of the women—dances—architecture of the villages—alarming property of wooden houses—agricultural customs—Novgorod—Valdai—Tver—Torjok—its staple manufactures of veal cutlets and morocco slippers—military road—Russian soldiers—arrival at Moscow.

"An English traveller," saith Mr. Josiah Conder, in his Modern Traveller, "who had visited the most remote and desolate parts of the Scottish Highlands, even half a century ago, would be ill-prepared to encounter the inconveniences, discomforts, and privations, to which he would be exposed in journeying from one capital of Russia to the other, if he did not carry along with him the means of preventing or remedying them. The representations of Dr. Clarke with regard to the condition of

Russia must be taken with much caution and quali-
fication; yet he speaks but the language of all other
travellers in this country, when he advises that nothing should be expected from inns, or houses of
entertainment, not even clean straw for a bed. He
enumerates the following articles as forming an
indispensable portion of the traveller's baggage:—a
pewter tea-pot; a kettle; a saucepan, the top of
which may be used as a dish; tea, sugar, and a
large cheese; loaves of bread made into rusks; if
in the winter, frozen meat; wine in the cold districts, vinegar in the hot. Thus prepared, he may
safely encounter this long journey."

This *crux viatorum* was not held forth in the
days of Peter the Great, but in the year 1825;
and, nevertheless, I had the courage to get into
the diligence at St. Petersburg, without any other
provision for so tremendous a journey than a bottle
of Cognac. The advantage of providing myself with
the said Cognac was twofold. In the first place,
the article—which is well-known to be the only
orthodox comforter of wayfaring men—is difficult to
be had on this road; and, in the second place, the
wine which is offered as a substitute is not sold in
small bottles: and I hope the reader agrees with
me that a large bottle would be too much at a time
—if taken very often in the day.

I found the road excellent; the inns, with few
exceptions, exceedingly comfortable; and the living,
good or bad as I chose: for the traveller dines by
the carte, and has the best wines of France and

Germany at his command. I should like to see a gentleman going into one of these establishments with a large cheese under his arm, and the lid of a saucepan by way of a dish. As for his kettle and pewter tea-pot, they would excite a universal cachinnation, spreading from village to village ; for almost every hut is provided with an immense tea-urn of burnished brass. In fact, the only discomfort or privation I suffered,—or, at least, was about to suffer,—was in the way of tea. I, in my unhappy ignorance, fancied the article to be exceedingly good; but a Russian merchant, one of my fellow-travellers, held my hand in time, warning me that it was destitute of the true oriental aroma. At every station he produced a secret hoard of his own, and insisted upon treating the company.

They drink much finer tea in Russia than in England ; but the difference, I suspect, does not lie in the land or sea carriage. In the former country, you meet with no such thing as five, or six, or seven shilling tea in a respectable house, whether public or private. The lowest price is ten or twelve rubles a pound—and the Russian pound is smaller than the English—from which rate it ascends to a guinea. At these prices I have a notion the tea is as good in London as any where else in the world.

The villagers between the two capitals must not be taken as a fair sample of the Russian peasantry. On this great highway, many circumstances contribute to enrich, and many to demoralize them. The women are often handsome,—setting aside the

peculiarity of shape which I noticed at St. Petersburg,—but, with hardly an exception, they are given
to the odious practice of painting their faces. This
blackens and destroys the teeth, and makes an
otherwise pretty face altogether unapproachable.
The custom, so far as I know, is entirely laid aside
by the nobility.

Every day appeared to me to be a holiday. In
the evening nothing was to be heard but music, and
nothing seen but groups of peasant-girls, magnificently
dressed, dancing and singing the Korovoda.

The musical instruments in the hands of the
Russian peasants are all extremely simple, and such
as correspond with the condition of a rude people.
Antiquarians trace most of them to the Greeks ;
but the musical instruments of one country may
resemble those of another, and yet be original in
both. Almost all nations, for instance, have invented a drum and a flute ; because these simple
contrivances for the production of musical sounds
will be stumbled upon accidentally, if the inventive
genius does not exist. The ancient Greek music is
in the same way said to be re-produced among the
forests of Russia ; but, in fact, the Russian melo-
dies bear a still greater resemblance to the national
airs of the Scots.

However, the learned Thebans behold the Cetra
of the ancients, described by Ovid, in the *balalayka*
of the Russian peasant. It is a sort of guitar, made
of hollow wood, the barrel part extremely small, and
furnished sometimes with two, sometimes with three

strings. It is neatly formed, but may be bought in Moscow for sixpence.

The Doudka is a flute.

The Gelaika is a double flute, resembling the one described by Horace.

The Gusli is a kind of piano, laid upon a table; and is furnished with steel chords touched by the fingers.

These, with the Pandean pipes, are all the ancient instruments of the Russians; and it does not appear that any attempt was ever made to improve them.

The vocal music resembles very much the Scottish, but has still less variety. The peasants go on for hours together ringing the changes upon a few notes, which would appear ridiculous if set down in the musical score; but when sung by them are touching and pleasing in no ordinary degree. In the article of *bells*, however, their taste is very extraordinary. They appear to have no idea of ringing harmony from such machines. They have a kind of music in which each performer takes only a single note, and thus a complete whole, instead of being woven together, is produced by separate and distinct sounds: yet it does not seem to occur to them that harmony may be extracted in the same manner from the conflicting tones of bell-metal. To live in the neighbourhood of a church in this country is distracting; for three or four bells, all of different calibres, are set clattering, and jarring, and thundering at the same instant, and will continue at such barbarous amusement for an hour together.

If Dr. Collins is to be believed, the change in musical taste since his time is not the least remarkable part of the revolution which has taken place in manners.

"In short," says he, "if you would please a Russian with musick, get a concert of Billingsgate nightingales, which joyned with a flight of screech owls, a nest of jackdaws, a pack of hungry wolves, seven hogs in a windy day, and as many cats with their carrivols, and let them sing Lacrymæ, and that will ravish a pair of Russian luggs better than all the musick in Italy, light ayres in France, marches of England, or the jigs of Scotland."

In the present day, the music is rich and pathetic, and the voices that sing it almost always rich and sweet. I am tempted to introduce here the following translation (as literally as it could be rendered) of a popular song. For this translation, also, I am indebted to Mr. J. C——.

> The white day is waning, the night cometh on,
> The night cometh on, and the twilight is fading;
> And to me, youthful one, my beloved sendeth,
> My beloved sendeth, and then cometh himself.
> "Art at home, my beloved, my own precious delight?"
> And I, youthful one, starting up in a flutter,
> I leap from my bed, and put on my shoes,
> Just to go into the balcony, just to whisper a word.
> I asked him first of his health—my dear, my beloved,
> And then I told him all, all his poor girl's grief.
> "O my bright falcon, my beautiful youth!
> Is it thus we must part?—even so must thou leave me?"
> "Even so, even so; and whilst thou, my charmer,
> Clasping thy hands, rainest tears on my face!"
> "Farewell, my beloved; farewell, my precious one!"

And I, youthful one, have a little green garden;
And in my little garden there are three trees.
On one tree there are sweet apples, on another green pears,
And the third, it is a bitter, bitter aspen.
On the aspen, there singeth a cuckoo among the branches.
Hark how the cuckoo singeth—" My sweet one complains,
She hath lost, she hath lost, him whose lips did kiss her!
She hath lost, she hath lost, him whose arms did fold her!"
Farewell, my beloved! Farewell, my precious one!

In this, however, there is too much poetry to allow me to think that it is a genuine song of the peasantry; and, besides, it is destitute of allusion to their peculiar customs and avocations. The following is a literal version of one of the Korovoda songs, which I heard so often as to make me familiar with many of the words, as well as with the air :—

A KOROVODA SONG.

" 'Tis millet we've sown, 'tis millet we've sown,
Oi Dida and Lado, have sown, have sown;
And the millet we'll tread, and the millet we'll tread;
Oi Dida and Lado, we'll tread, we'll tread."

" But with what will you tread? Oh, with what will you tread?
Oi Dida and Lado, with what will you tread?"

" With horses let loose, with horses let loose;
Oi Dida and Lado, with horses let loose.
And the horses we'll catch, the horses we'll catch,
Oi Dida and Lado, we'll catch, we'll catch."

" But, with what will you catch, with what will you catch?
Oi Dida and Lado, will catch, will catch?"

"Oh! with nets of silk, and with nets of silk
Oi Dida and Lado, with nets, with nets.
Or the horses we'll buy, we'll buy, we'll buy;
Oi Dida and Lado, we'll buy, we'll buy."

Q 2

" But with what will you buy ?—with what will you buy ?
Oi Dida and Lado, will buy, will buy ?"

" We'll give you a hundred, a hundred rubles ;
Oi Dida and Lado, a hundred, a hundred."

" A thousand wo'nt do, not a thousand will do,
Oi Dida and Lado, a thousand, a thousand !"

" Then we'll give a young lass, a fair young lass,
Oi Dida and Lado, a pretty young lass."

" That—*that* is the price—'tis that we must have,
Oi Dida and Lado, 'tis that we must have."

The above simple ditty is not only connected with the every-day avocations of the peasantry, but with their ancient paganism. The festival of the Slavonian goddess Dida, and her son Lado, was celebrated by the songs of the devotees as they circled round a birchen-tree in one of the slow dances of their country. The tree was hung with ribbons, which were afterwards thrown into the river, and auguries drawn from the forms they assumed in floating down the stream.

In performing the Korovoda, the peasant girls join hands in a circle ; but, instead of a birchen-tree, they have the smartest lass, or best singer in the village, in the middle. The motions of the dance, if dance it can be called, are slow and languid, and the air is extremely simple and almost melancholy. The song, notwithstanding, appears to amuse the performers very much ; the most waggish smiles and glances are interchanged ; and, at the conclusion, when the priestess selects another young

girl, and draws her into the middle, the men who
are looking on invariably hail the consummation
with a loud laugh. I must add, that the heathenish
names of Dida and Lado are beginning to be
omitted in some districts; the priests having admonished their simple flock that to pronounce them
is a sin.

I was very much surprised by the holiday garb
of the peasant girls on this road; which was as rich
in appearance as it must have been expensive in
reality. Some wore a garment resembling the large
cape of a man's cloak, drawn in or not at the waist
at the fancy of the wearer. This was always of silk
or satin, lined with lambs'-wool as white as snow.
Some looked still better in the national sarafan,
likewise of the same rich materials; and, in this
case, their shirt sleeves, very full and dazzlingly
white, reaching to the wrist, gave them the appearance of ladies of the court. Sometimes these garments were embroidered with gold lace; and almost
always the shoes either glittered with spangles, or
were made of morocco leather of different colours.
Their ear-rings were generally in the form of a
triangle, and of real pearls—a fact which at first I
could hardly bring myself to believe. The curiosity
I expressed appeared to gratify these simple girls
very much; and, with a kindness and politeness
native to the Russian female, they allowed me to
examine their ear-rings and capotes as much as I
chose.

The men rarely joined in the amusements of the

women, although they sometimes crowded round
them to look on. Singing in parts seemed to be
their own favourite recreation; but sometimes they
performed the strange dance peculiar to their country. This was described by Olearius as consisting
of various slow movements of the head and shoulders, while the feet remained almost stationary; and,
to the present day, no alteration whatever has taken
place. The individuals who appeared to me to
be the fondest of this amusement were the soldiers;
and a circle of these men, wrapped in their grey
cloaks, watching with the deepest interest the performance of a single comrade, formed a highly
curious spectacle. The women, in the meantime,
only a few yards off, pursued their Korovoda,
neither party taking the smallest notice of each
other. Maltebrun says, after some traveller, that
the Russians are as great dancers as the French;
but this is altogether incorrect.

The houses in the villages, with a very few
exceptions, are of wood, that is to say, built of pine-
trees, stripped of the bark, and laid horizontally
upon each other. They are generally of two stories,
standing with their gable-ends to the road, the roof
projecting some distance, and often ornamented with
rude sculpture. At each story, there are two,
three, and even four small glazed windows,
placed in a line. A strong prejudice prevails
in favour of wooden houses, which are said to be
warmer and wholesomer than those of brick or
stone. At one time of the year, however, a stranger

to their peculiarities runs some risk of getting a severe fright. When a sudden thaw takes place, a terrific noise is heard throughout the building, giving the idea, if it occurs in the night time, of a band of robbers attempting to burst into the house. A friend of mine, Mr. F——— of Moscow, on one occasion of the kind, leaped from his bed, armed himself with his pistols, and remained in great alarm for a considerable time.

In 1804 there were eighty-seven millions of pines in Russia fit for building; and at the same period there were eight millions proper to be used for masts.

Till reaching Novgorod I found the agricultural habits of the peasants pretty nearly the same as those in Finland. During a part of the route they dry the grain in the same way, and are thus able to keep it, if necessary, for fifteen or even eighteen years. The custom of burning the trees for the sake of manure is also the same. I have myself repeatedly seen the operation in the governments of St. Petersburg and Novgorod.*

In some districts they throw the seeds into the almost hot ashes as soon as the fire is extinct. The time chosen is when the dew of the evening falls; and, going over the ground with nothing else than a slight plough and a wooden rake, it sometimes produces, it is said, even a hundred fold. It is remarked

---

* Not on the present journey. I was subsequently on this road, and have thrown the observations made at both times into one.

that the peasants, as is natural in the case of ignorant persons, are so fond of these large and quick
returns, that they leave uncultivated the really good
land. Their triumph lasts, however, only for three
years—and in some cases the crops are pretty good
even for four or five years; but after that, the land
which has thus been manured with its own ashes,
and fed upon its own substance, is good for nothing
for twenty years to come.

Novgorod is a very interesting city to the Russian
antiquary—if Russia can be said to have any thing
to do with antiquity at all. It must be studied,
however, in its history, not in its monuments,
Even when worth preserving, the perishing nature of
the materials sets it out of the question; and the
traveller will be perfectly well satisfied with the
space—always too ample—allowed him by the conducteur of the diligence for inspecting the remains
of Novgorod the Great.

The cathedral of Saint Sophia is considered one
of the oldest churches in Russia; and there are also
several others built of brick. The city was once a
Hanseatic town, and contained a population of four
hundred thousand souls. It still occupies a large
area of ground; but its inhabitants amount only to
six or seven thousand. Its grandeur began to
decline at the commencement of the fifteenth century; and the foundation of St. Petersburg
destroyed all the little consequence it had then
left.

Valdai is a small town which stands in one of the

best situations on this road. The country around may even be said to be romantic; and the place itself is celebrated both for its bells and belles; the former having the sweetest tones, and the latter the fairest faces in this part of the country.

Tver is an important town, where the barks pass into the canal of Vichney-Volochik for the Volga. But I must not forget to say, that at Torjok I had the satisfaction of eating the finest *veal cutlets* in Europe. Every body knows the veal cutlets of Torjok, and the French lady who manufactures them; and every body has heard her account of the praises bestowed upon them by the whole world. This praise, indeed, was so loud and long, that the empress herself burned with curiosity to taste them; and madame had the honour of being brought to St. Petersburg express, to make veal cutlets for majesty.

Another celebrated manufacture of Torjok is that of morocco slippers, caps, &c. &c. The leather is in different pieces of different colours, stitched together with silk, and forming various agreeable figures ornamented with gold and silver lace.

I do not think that on this road the scenery is so bad, or the route so uninteresting as travellers in general assert; but I have a great deal to do within the little space that is left to me, and must hurry on to Moscow. It ought to be said, however, that the road itself is excellent from beginning to end. At regular distances it is severed by a deep and wide trench, which is crossed by means of a wooden bridge, making a sharp turn to the right or left.

This bridge, in case of the march of an enemy, could either be destroyed or defended; and, from the great number of such interventions occurring in the space of four hundred and eighty-seven miles between the two cities, a serious annoyance would be opposed to the progress of the invading force.

There is also to be seen at the road-side every few versts an object less easily comprehended by the stranger. It is a small but handsomely painted house, with an esplanade carefully rolled, and an unarmed soldier standing sentry like a statue at the door. On the esplanade there is a large wooden triangular machine, brilliantly painted, and the traveller, not knowing what else to do with it, sets it down as some unheard-of engine of punishment. Its real purpose, however, is merely to clear the road of the snow; and the whole military establishment is devoted to similar objects.

The Russian soldiers are far from being formidable in appearance. At St. Petersburg, the Guards, who are in general almost the only force there, are drawn in at the waist like wasps, till they can hardly breathe; and so helpless do they seem, that the idea occurred to me when looking along the line, that by means of a single good buffet on the ear of the nearest man the whole rank might be floored. Out of St. Petersburg, they are, taking them in the mass, small, mean-looking, shuffling fellows. Their undress is peculiarly unbecoming; and even in warm weather you see them shambling along, buttoned up to the throat in

coarse grey greatcoats. When they spy an officer
on the road, even at a considerable distance, they
pull off their bonnet, and do not presume to put it
on again till they are far beyond his reach. The
officer on his part, however low be his rank, and
although when in undress almost as shabby as the
men, hardly ever deigns the smallest salutation.

When a peasant is enlisted he becomes nominally
free, and may even rise to promotion; but before
this takes place, he appears to me to be looked upon
by his superiors rather as a peasant than a soldier.
This is partly owing, no doubt, to the scantiness of
his pay, which obliges him to undertake any menial
job he can get. In the towns a general fund
arising from such resources is under the care of
one of the officers, and divided by him among the
men.

When on military duty, however, these fellows
change their character. In St. Petersburg they
march on the pavement, not in Indian file, but as
many abreast as will exactly fill the space, and
compel the other passengers to flounder in the mud
of the street. This is an intolerable hardship in the
spring, when it is impossible to cross a street without
wading ankle-deep. I had one day the misfortune
to meet an entire regiment in this way; and when I
insisted upon planting myself at the wall, while they
passed, instead of in the mud, they seemed astonished
at my impudence.

I arrived at Moscow on the fourth night after
leaving St. Petersburg; and as it was too late

R

to obtain entrance into the hotels, I availed myself of the hospitality extended to travellers by government, and stretched myself upon a sofa in the post-house.

CHAPTER XII.

FROM almost the earliest epoch of its history, Russia formed a kind of federation of States, very slightly connected in a political sense, but yet all feeling that they belonged to the same country. The princes of these states vied with each other for the empty title of grand or supreme prince ; a name which, during the long period of the Tatar domination, simply meant, first slave and vassal of the Mongol. The wars of these petty chiefs are uninteresting in

the sameness of their atrocity; and here it only
needs to be said, that in the latter half of the
fourteenth century, the title in dispute seems to
have become definitively attached to the dukedom of
Moscow.   In 1432 the first prince was crowned in
that city, and Vladimir, where the coronation ceremony had hitherto taken place, fell from its rank of
capital.

In 1547 Moscow was already a great city, since it
lost in one conflagration upwards of seventeen
hundred lives.   It was then built of wood; and
even the inclosures of the gardens being of the same
material, the very trees were converted into char-
coal.   In 1602 it had waxed prodigiously; for then
it was able to lose a hundred and twenty-seven
thousand individuals by a pestilence.   In 1636,
according to the testimony of Olearius, it was "one
of the greatest cities in Europe," containing no
fewer than two thousand churches.   The streets
were very broad; but the houses being of wood,
fires were so frequent that men were stationed every
where with pole-axes to cut down, in case of need,
the adjoining buildings.   Such is the origin of the
watchmen of to-day.   Under Alexis, the father of
Peter the Great, the houses were still almost all
of wood, sometimes tapestried with Flemish leather.
The foundation of St. Petersburg eventually
deprived the city of much of its ancient importance;
and in 1812 it was almost totally destroyed in consequence of the invasion of the French.

The Moscow of to-day, therefore, is a new city;

with fragments here and there of the ancient skeleton, enough to plunge the traveller into a reverie, and fill the busy precincts around him with the shapes that in general haunt only tombs and ruins.

I cannot account for the circumstance; but since I have heard the same thing remarked in conversation by others, I may venture to mention, that if I had left Moscow on the second or third day after my arrival, I should have pronounced it to be far inferior in interest to St. Petersburg. It did not at first strike me with the surprise I should expect from the novelty of its details when I now remember them; and I turned away almost with weariness from a view, exhibiting at one instant between thirteen and fourteen hundred domes, spires, and cupolas.

If this is strange, the forcible manner in which the scene afterwards took hold of my imagination is still stranger. Day after day, hour after hour, it fixed, and grappled, and clung. I wandered, like an unquiet spirit, about the streets; I gazed from the esplanade of the Kremlin—from the tower of Ivan Velikoi—from the Shivoy Gorka—and still the cravings of my curiosity were unsatisfied. After a residence of six weeks, I left Moscow with the *sacra fames* unappeased; and to this day the Holy City rises upon my dreams like a vision of poetry or romance.

Moscow may have been injured in its trade by the foundation of the new metropolis; it may have been shorn of its wealth by the invasion of Napoleon : but so long as the Russians retain their character as a distinct people, so long as they worship the gods of their forefathers, it will still be the dearest haunt of their steps, it will still be the HOLY CITY. Its soil is enriched with the blood of martyrs ; its temples are filled with the bones of the saints. It is the East of the soul, to which men turn in prayer. When St. Petersburg herself desires more especially to sanctify her ceremonies and processions, she sends to this elder sister to borrow some of those inestimable relics, without whose presence the sparkle of gold and gems would be less than nothing and vanity.

To see the look of the wandering peasant when he approaches Moscow !—when, yet afar off, the sound of her thousand bells is wafted upon his ear ! —when the proud and beautiful spectacle of her towers, and domes, and spires, unfolds itself to his eye ! He pauses—he, this untamed savage, this creature of the senses of the perishing body—in a tumult of awe, affection, and delight ! He pulls off his hat, makes the sign of the cross upon his brow, shoulders, and bosom, clasps his hands upon his chest, and bows his body to the earth. He advances another step towards the Holy City ; and then sinks upon his knees, and falls down upon his face, touching the ground with his forehead.

On the Sparrow Hills, where the French army saw for the first time the devoted city, a splendid view is obtained—perhaps one of the richest views

From the Mecklenburgh Gardens.

of the kind in Europe ; but too extensive for an ordinary sized engraving. Mr. Vickers, therefore, has chosen a part of the Nieskooshni gardens. The Moskva is in front, with one of the long rafts of the country floating down the stream ; and, in the distance, the city rises above the horizon, with the tall tower of Ivan Velikoi overtopping the whole.

From this place the ground on which it stands appears to be almost a flat ; but, as we advance towards it, from the rising and falling of the parts of the picture, we perceive that, in reality, the city stands upon lofty ground, swelling from the water's edge, and variegated with numerous eminences. The nature of the site alone gives it an advantage over the new capital ; for, every now and then, as you wander on, a different point of view is obtained, and the town presents itself in a different aspect. These aspects, however, are different only when you have been long enough here to recollect yourself. For the first day or two you are bewildered, probably fatigued, by the mass of domes and cupolas rising on all sides around you. It is not till you recover from this confusion of mind, and are able in some degree to arrange and classify the objects around, that you feel the whole effect of Moscow.

But, when you approach these buildings, which so astonish you in the mass, a new sensation altogether is produced. You find yourself—perhaps, for the first time, however much you may have travelled—in a strange and far-away land, in such a place as hitherto you have only seen in the clouds, when a rich sun-set brings out in sharp light and shadow, a thousand gay, gorgeous, grotesque, and unworldly forms.

To describe in words the innumerable temples of of the HOLY CITY, or any one of them, is altogether impossible. A new language would be required, a new nomenclature. They possess nothing in common with the other temples of the world; or, sometimes, even with one another. In this case, the pencil is worth a thousand pens; and a glance at the opposite page will do more to enable the reader to form an idea of a Muscovite church than a whole volume of description. But still the imagination must have its share of the employment, as well as the eyes. A great part of the effect produced by the architecture of Moscow lies in the colouring; and you must daub that fantastic pile all over with red, yellow, blue, green, silver, and gold, before it looks half as fantastic as it is.

This, however, is not a common specimen taken at random from the mass. It is ultra-Russian in taste. It is the famous cathedral of Vassili Blagennoi; with which its founder, Ivan the Terrible, was so much delighted, that he is said to have put out the architect's eyes, in order that it might remain the chef d'œuvre of his art. This story, however, I do not believe. The church was founded in 1554, in memory of the conquest of Kazan, and the tsaritsa Anastasia did not die till 1560. Ivan had not yet become the Terrible to his own subjects; for his good angel, that amiable and lovely princess, had not yet taken her flight to heaven.

Another class of buildings are the palaces of the nobility, and the hospitals and hospices. These are in the taste of St. Petersburg, and they imitate in the same way the classic models. They are all of some light and delicate colour. Between are frequently small, or undistinguished houses ; but these, too, are painted to correspond. The effect of the city, therefore, is unique in the whole, although as different as may be in its separate parts.

The houses are in general low ; in very rare cases containing more than two stories, and very often consisting entirely of a rez de chaussée. In the part of the town called the Zemlenoï-gorod, and in the faubourgs, they are usually built of wood ; but every where else brick is the material, interspersed with deals as at St. Petersburg. For the foundations, however, stone is used ; a very scarce and dear article. It is brought either from the quarries of Tartarovo, which are already nearly exhausted, or from Mitchkova, several leagues from the city.

We find the scarcity of stones existing even in the time of Alexis, father of Peter the Great. When the famous boiar Matveef was at length persuaded by his friend the emperor to build himself a new house, the work was at a stand for want of materials for the foundation. As soon as this was publicly known, the citizens assembled, and Matveef saw carts arriving from all quarters filled with stones. He demanded the price.

" These stones," said they, " are not for sale. We have taken them from the tombs of our fathers to present to our benefactor !"

" What shall I do, my prince ?" said the boiar, in agitation.

" Take them," replied the tsar ; " were such a gift offered to me, God knows how proud I should be to accept of it !"

The tomb of Matveef is in the street of the Armenians, where it was erected by Count Romanzof, one of his descendants. It is too simple, for it wants the magnitude which makes simplicity grand. The illustrious boiar, after having been banished by court intrigues to one of the dreariest districts in the country of Archangel, found, on his return, the whole capital convulsed by the revolt of the Strelits; and he fell by their hands, a victim to his courage and loyalty.

Before the conflagration of Moscow in 1812, there were nine thousand one hundred and fifty-eight houses, of which six thousand three hundred and forty-one were destroyed. In another place will be seen a table containing a statement of the present number of buildings, by which it will be observed that the city has already—in the space of twenty-five years—regained more than it lost.

The pavement of the streets is formed of pebbles taken from the bed of the Moskva, and comprising specimens of jaspers and other stones interesting to the mineralogist, but peculiarly obnoxious to the pieton. There are in general trottoirs, however, more carefully paved, even when the same in materials.

The pietons are in general far more interesting than those of St. Petersburg. We see here the Russian merchant in all his glory. He still belongs, indeed, to a caste separate from that of the nobility, but he is no longer ashamed of it. He does not live in a city of the nobles, where he must find himself the slave of their wants and wishes; for the number at Moscow is comparatively small, and they are in general invested with so much historical dignity that the reverence they demand involves no degradation. This idea assumes no form in the merchant's brain, but he is conscious of it notwithstanding. He begins to talk of "his order." On great occasions he walks majestically through the streets in a uniform covered with gold lace; for the emperor, with a far-sighted policy worthy of Peter the Great himself, has offered a premium upon pride.

The merchant's wife is rarely seen in the streets; but when she is, you make room for her with involuntary respect. She is dressed in a robe of silk or satin so rich in the materials, and so exquisitely delicate, or so gorgeously bright in the colour, that it might serve for a queen. Her face is beautiful, for she is painted with such art that one requires to approach very close indeed to discover the counterfeit; and her dark bright eyes wander about, or rest upon yours, with all the curiosity which is natural in a recluse. In order that you should not mistake her for a noblewoman, she wears upon her head a little sad-coloured silk handkerchief, put on with such artful simplicity, that the very ties are concealed.

The merchant's son is a tall good-humoured looking fellow, sometimes with a smoothly shaven chin, and sometimes with a little beard that offers a compromise between his own modern taste and his sire's antique prejudices. He wears no sash, and his caftan begins to sneak stealthily into the European frock.

The merchant's daughter is a little girl with a French bonnet, a muslin gown, and bishop's sleeves. You can see with one eye that she reads French novels and plays the piano. She does not walk beside her papa and mamma, but either after or before them. Neither does she take her brother's arm. She has a pensive air, like one who thinks much; and sometimes, in a fit of abstraction, will allow her eye to rest upon yours for half a minute at a time.

The artificers of the town are like those of St. Petersburg, and generally wear long boots; but almost all the other mujiks are in shoes of the linden bark. The women of this class are almost as numerous as the men; for if they do not come in from the country to work, they come to pray. Nearly every day there are processions of twenty—thirty—forty—or fifty peasant women passing through the streets, dressed in coarse gowns of a drab colour, with wallets at their back and long staves in their hand. These are pilgrims; and

after worshipping in the Holy City, it is probably
their intention to go on to the famous monastery of
Troitsa, at a distance of eighty versts. In this case
in addition to the linden shoes on their feet, they
have a pair dangling at their waist; for they must
walk every step of the way, or lose the benefit of
their devotion. These women are of all ages above
fifteen or sixteen, and of all complexions; but their
shapeless gown, and their short petticoats displaying
rags wrapped about their legs instead of stockings,
confer upon them an appearance altogether unat-
tractive.

In a city of temples like this, the monks and
priests, it may be supposed, form no inconsiderable
part of the population; but in addition to them
there are here numerous nuns. These are not shut
up in their convents as in Catholic countries; but,
dressed in black from top to toe, with high conical
caps, and unveiled faces, they form rather an
interesting part of the street picturesque.

All the above classes are natives; but the foreigners
are so numerous as to play a very prominent part in
the show. At St. Petersburg they are distinguished by their pig-tailed coats, jerking gait, and
smooth chins; while here we see every modification
of the oriental physiognomy, costume, and manner.
The Tatars, Persians, and Armenians are the most
numerous, great multitudes of them residing
habitually at Moscow, where they have places of
worship of their own; but in addition to these the
Turkish provinces, the Krimea, the Caucasus, all

have their representatives. This central city of Russia is a point of union between the White Sea and the Frozen Ocean on the North, and the Euxine, the Sea of Azof, and the Caspian on the south; between the Sea of Okotsk on the east, and the Baltic and the Gulf of Bothnia on the west. Merchants congregate here from all quarters; and travellers meet, to stare at one another, from the Thames, the Nile, the Ganges, and the Mississippi.

On my arrival, the whole of this variegated population were stirring like the inhabitants of a bee-hive. There seemed to be a "sensation" in the town, as if something prodigious had happened—as if another Alexandrine column was erecting itself in the Kremlin.

"The emperor is come!"—this was the cry; and the nobles were yoking their coaches and four, the droskis flying, double loaded, along the streets, and the mujiks, male and female, rushing like a whirlwind after. At St. Petersburg, where the emperor habitually resides, he is a man of—considerably upwards of six feet; but nothing more. He reviews his troops before the palace, goes out to walk with his wife and children, strolls along the English quay, and although every hat is moved that is in the way, very few come on purpose to move. And why?—because they can come at any time.

In Moscow he is a rarity; in Moscow, which is a *Russian* city, he is beloved almost to idolatry.

"Our little father!" cry the mujiks, looking up

into his face with devoted affection as he struggles through them.

"Come now, make a little room for me," says the emperor, passing on with his hand raised to his hat, "do, brother, stand out of the way!" The occasion is like a fête through the whole town, and the Kremlin, to which every body has access, is like the scene of a great fair. The palace, defended from the people by no enclosure, is surrounded by a dense crowd of men, women, and children, from morning till night. Sometimes a beautiful little boy, one of the young princes climbs up to the window to look out, and all heads are instantly uncovered as if he was Nicolas himself.

One day the imperial mother of this really fine family was sitting at the window, looking down upon the crowd, when the emperor coming behind her, put his arm round her neck and kissed her. No one unacquainted with the Russian character can conceive the effect of this simple act. The general shout that came from the lips of the people arose from the holiest depths of their heart; and I venture to say, that there was no man of that vast concourse who would not have laid down his life for the Tsar, and no woman who would not have urged her son or husband to do so.

I have mentioned the arrival of their majesties, only as it was connected with the more than usually picturesque attitude in which I found the town; but perhaps it may be as well to conclude this chapter with the very little I mean to say on the subject of

their private character.   It was my wish to have
been presented to the emperor *by chance;* but a
circumstance unknown to the kind friend at St.
Petersburg who furnished me with letters of recom-
mendation for that purpose, prevented my ambition
from being gratified.   Prince S. G——, however,
had the goodness to offer me a formal presentation
through the governor-general; but the ceremony,
uninteresting in itself, has been described so often
that I did not think it worth the suit of uniform it
would have cost.

The emperor, who is a very tall and a very
handsome man, is naturally of a lively disposition.
He is always dressed with great precision, and every
one understands that it is necessary to appear before
him both well dressed and with a cheerful countenance.   He is easy of access; and seems to think an
appearance of state almost unnecessary.   At St.
Petersburg, however, at each side of the door which
leads to the imperial apartments, stands a black
man gorgeously dressed in eastern costume.   There
are twelve of these men, who relieve each other
alternately in the duty of opening and shutting the
door, and announcing the name of the visitor.

After breakfast the emperor's first care is to go to
the nursery to see his children, and ascertain how
they have slept.   He takes each of them up, kisses
them, romps with them—for he is full of frolic, and
glad to be a boy again when the cares of the world
will let him.

Their majesties dine at three o'clock (the general

hour for the upper classes in Russia) with perfect simplicity; and towards the conclusion of the meal, the Grand Duke Alexander and the younger children come in to kiss their parents. When they rise from table, the emperor bestows upon his consort, also, some hearty kisses. He calls her " his wife ;" but the empress, who is a Prussian, never alludes to him but as " the emperor." She speaks English extremely well; but Nicolas only indifferently.

" The character of the emperor and empress," writes an English friend to me, " is such that it is difficult to speak of them without exciting in strangers a suspicion that the description is overcharged. It is no exaggeration to say, that I never saw a family where *more* affection and harmony existed, and that I believe the examples to be very rare indeed where *so much* can be discovered. I have frequently seen these illustrious individuals surrounded by their children, and have partaken of the influence every one receives who witnesses the scene ; and I can say, that in their domestic virtues they are worthy of being held forth as a pattern not only to all sovereigns but to all mankind."

At St. Petersburg, Nicolas has frequently gone home in a droski when it rained ; and once having no money in his pocket, the isvoschik, ignorant of his quality, detained his cloak till he sent down the fare. A better anecdote, however, is told of the contact he sometimes comes into with the lower classes.

One Easter on coming out of the palace he

addressed the sentry with his usual familiarity, in the form of salutation prescribed for that day— "Christ is risen!" Instead of the usual reply, "He is indeed," the fellow answered gravely, "He is *not* indeed!"

"Hey? how? what is that?" said the emperor, "I said, Christ is risen!"

"And I replied, He is *not!*"

"Why, who and what, in God's name, are you?"

"*I am a Jew.*"

CHAPTER XIII.

Origin of Moscow—Kremlin—bazaar town—white town—
earthen town—holy gate—nunnery of the Ascension—tower
of Ivan Velikoi—cathedral of the Annunciation—grand
cathedral—Virgin of Vladimir—convent of Miracles—
curious superstition—general effect of the scene—treasury—
catalogue raisonné of street dainties—rarity of drunkenness
—excesses in tobacco committed only by the genteel.

In ancient times, say the antiquaries, the banks
of the Moskva at a certain place were covered with
a gloomy forest. In the middle of this forest was a
marsh, and in the middle of the marsh a little island,
where a hermit whose name was Boukal built himself a hut. In process of years the hermit disappeared, and there arose on the spot a *kremle*,
which is the Tatar word for fortress, and his hut
was replaced by a palace.

The Kremlin, forming an irregular polygon surrounded by lofty walls, flanked by towers at the angles, was the original Moscow. It was surrounded by a ditch, formed of the waters of the little river Neglinna, which came hither to discharge itself into the Moskva. This stream is now condemned to find its way in the dark, being vaulted over; and above its bed, the citizens wander, or recline, in the most beautiful promenades that were ever seen in the centre of a great city.

Numerous shops and markets speedily arose to the east of the future metropolis, [and without the walls; and in 1534 these were considerable enough to be surrounded by a ditch, and in the following year by a wall of their own. This portion of the town, which is called the Kitaï-gorod, stands together with the Kremlin, on the left bank of the Moskva, where the river forms a broad serpentine fold.

A still more extensive faubourg arose on the same bank of the river, embracing the whole breadth of the angle, and surrounding the two former portions except at the water side. It is called the Beloï-gorod, or white town, probably from its walls having been built of a white stone. They have now disappeared, and are replaced by a planted boulevard.

The last faubourg was the Zemlenoï-gorod, or earthern town, so called from a rampart which surrounded it, and which is now replaced by planted promenades. It forms a complete circle round the others on both sides of the river.

Drawn by A.G. Vickers.

Engraved by H. Jorden.

The Folly gate and walls of the Kremlin.

MOSCOW

London, Published Oct.ʳ 1, 1835, for the Proprietors, by Longman & Cº Paternoster Row, Bissner & Cº Paris, Albert Berlin.

The streets and houses which extend beyond this quarter, and to which no general name is attached, although they are surrounded by a rampart, form a very irregular figure; making the greatest length of the city thirteen versts and two hundred and thirty feet, its greatest breadth eight versts and two hundred and ten feet, and its circumference about forty versts.

The Kremlin, although the smallest quarter, is undoubtedly the most worthy of attention; and as the engravings that accompany these pages relate almost exclusively to this extraordinary mass of architecture, the reader will be able to form almost as good an idea of the place as if he was himself on the spot. In filling in the colouring, however, he must not be so lavish as I have recommended on a former occasion. The buildings of the Kremlin are with few exceptions white, and the domes and cupolas of the churches golden. For this reason, as well as from their form, the fantastic character of the scene is united with wonderful lightness and elegance.

The walls are faithfully and beautifully described in the series of engravings. They are embattled in their whole length; and it will be observed, that however odd and original are the towers by which they are flanked, the prevailing order is Gothic. In the plate annexed the Spaskoï, or Holy Gate, conducts us direct into the middle of the group of palaces and cathedrals. Every one who enters by this gate must take off his hat while traversing the

passage—for the place is holy. The origin of the
custom is uncertain; some dating it from the last
pestilence, and some from the deliverance of the city
from one of the Tatar invasions: but the Russians
hold fast by it with religious zeal, and the stranger
who errs from ignorance is instantly admonished by
the sentry.

On entering the gate the scene is splendid beyond
description. On the left the view is open. A part
of the esplanade is railed in for the exercise of the
troops, and beyond them, at a great depth, you see
the thousand domes of the city. On your right
stands the convent of the nuns of the Ascension,
adjoining the new palace, and in front are the tall
tower of Ivan Velikoi, and a numerous group of other
buildings surmounted by gilded domes and cupolas.
The convent contains two churches, one of which is
modern, and forms a nameless jumble of the Grecian
and Gothic. The establishment was founded in
1389, and contains the tombs of thirty-five grand
princesses. I have seen here one or two nuns who
might be called *almost* pretty; and that is far more
than can be said of the rest of the holy sisters in
Moscow. If the dress were made a little more
becoming, I have no doubt that we should see in
the nunneries a little more of the beauty of holiness.

On passing the convent and the new palace, there
are three buildings exactly in front. The one on
the left hand is the cathedral of Saint Michael the
Archangel; that on the right is Our Lady of
Pechersk, founded in thanksgiving for a victory

over the Tatars ; and that in the middle is the church of Saint Nicholas, with the tower of Ivan Velikoi.

The tower is isolated from the other buildings. It was erected in 1600, in the time of a frightful pestilence, by the poor of the city, who received bread in return for their labour. It is two hundred and sixty-six feet high, not including the cupola, which is thirty-seven, or the cross, which is eighteen. The cupola is plated with fine gold, the cross with gilded copper.

These buildings may be said to form one side of a square, the opposite side of which is formed by the palace of the tsars, the imperial palace, and the angular palace, with the cathedral of the Annunciation, and the grand cathedral of the Assumption between.

The former cathedral was almost renewed by Catharine II. in 1770 ; but its origin goes back to the end of the fourteenth century. Its appearance is " high fantastic ;" and its roof and nine cupolas being richly gilded, the whole presents an aspect of barbarian splendour unequalled even in Moscow. It is said, but I know not with what truth, that the cross of the centre cupola is of solid gold. The interior is small and dimly lighted, but full of the tawdry richness of the Greek church. The whole of the walls, both of the church and vestibule, are covered with frescoes representing sacred subjects. The saints, however, are mingled with the heathen philosophers, distinguished by their names ; and the latter hold in their hands little scrolls, written with sentences of the gospel! There are nine images, remarkable for sanctity and splendour; and these, as well as the other ornaments of the church, contained forty years ago upwards of eleven hundred pounds of silver, and upwards of seventy-seven pounds of gold. The pavement is of square agates.

The church of the Assumption is the grand cathedral of Moscow. It was founded in 1325; but the present edifice dates only from 1475, when it was constructed by a Bolognese architect. It has nothing Italian, however, in its form, and very little in its ornaments. The artist appears to have studied for his models, at least in general effect, the Russian monuments; although a writer in the Quarterly Review discovers the Saxon and Norman taste throughout.

In the interior, a view of which is annexed, the walls and columns of the church are covered with frescoes; but an image of the Virgin of Vladimir, *painted by the evangelist St. Luke,* is the grand ornament. A solitaire worn by this precious lady is valued at eighty thousand rubles, and the whole shrine at two hundred thousand. There are many images which, independently of their religious value, are highly curious as monuments of the arts. Here, also, were once the tombs of the patriarchs; and near the southern door is the ancient throne of the tsars. The ikonastas, ascending to the vaults, is one blaze of gold and vermilion.

Here are performed the most imposing ceremonies of the Greek church; and, if the tower of Ivan

Drawn by A. G. Vickers.

Engraved by T. Higham.

Interior of the grand Cathedral of the Assumption

Moscow.

Printed by Fenner & Fisher.

London, Published Oct.ʳ 1 1835, for the Proprietor, by Longman & Co. Paternoster Row, Bunce & Co. Paris, Asher, Berlin.

Velikoi is the centre of the city to the eye, the cathedral of the Assumption is of the same dignity to the heart.

So much has been said about the Great Bell in the space opposite that tower that I shall do nothing more than mention it. It is buried in the earth, and the place covered over with wood, through which you descend by a trap-door.

To the right of the bell, as you look towards the tower, and adjoining the new palace, is the Convent of Miracles. One of its churches is dedicated to Saint Michael, and the other to Saint Alexis; and both are handsome of the kind. On the outside of the wall there is a picture of the Trinity, which, on a front view, represents a dove, the symbol of the Holy Ghost. If you look from the right, you see a portrait of the Father; if from the left, one of the Son.

In one of these churches there is the dead body of the saint, with the skull exposed for the benefit of the faithful. I pressed forward, as usual, with the crowd, but was satisfied with a look. I turned away in horror from one of the most foul and dis-gusting objects I ever saw in my life; while my neighbours, male and female, kissed it with all the eagerness of an earthly attachment. I was happy however to be kept in countenance by the little children, who, when held down to print a holy salute upon the black and nasty-looking bones, signified by their squalls how distasteful it was. In these churches, as well as several others, some of

T

the images are to all appearance, if not in reality, graven images; the figures being raised in metal from the ikonastas in a kind of bas-relief, without painting. It is here, also, where the carved representation of the crucifixion which I have mentioned is to be seen with a candle burning before it.

In the little church of Saint John the Forerunner, at the western angle of the Kremlin, a curious superstition is permitted. There is a stone underneath the shrine of Saint Ouar, in which children are laid down who have some mortal disease. If it is the will of God to spare their lives, they recover: if not, they die instantaneously. Above the stone is hung a bunch of small crosses, such as are tied about the necks of children at their baptism. These, I was told, were gifts to the shrine from those who had thus miraculously escaped from the jaws of death; and I found, on counting them, that there were between thirty and forty.

I was not satisfied, however, with the story. I was loath to write down so grave an accusation against the Russian church at second hand; and I determined to witness the ceremony myself. An opportunity was not long of occurring. On going there one morning, I saw no fewer than six women with children at their breasts, waiting for the priest. On the arrival of the holy man, each woman went in in turn, heard a short prayer, kissed a crucifix which he held out to her, and held it to the wan lips of the infant. The priest's part was then over. He stepped aside to wait for another customer;

while the mother, laying down her charge upon the mystic stone, prostrated herself before the shrine. Her devotions over,—and they did not occupy more than a minute,—she took up the poor babe again, and retired. The church, therefore, I can say, takes no active share in this most paltry superstition ; it merely permits and encourages it.

The name of the saint means *heavy* ; and this is satisfactory enough reason for their having furnished him with a large stone. One of his old teeth, however, cures tooth-ache ; for what reason is not so plain. Saint Ouar suffered martyrdom in Egypt, in the year 296.

The palace of the tsars, and the angular palace, are buildings of the fifteenth century ; but they are rather grotesque than magnificent. In fact, it would be equally useless and difficult to give a minute description of the edifices of the Kremlin. It is the effect of the whole picture which is admirable—the towers, the domes, the cupolas, the golden roofs, the staircases, the balconies, the ornaments, Grecian, Gothic, Saxon, and Russian, all mingled together in wild confusion. The only apartment worth mentioning in any of the palaces is the throne room in the angular palace ; and this is worthy of mention only for its antique, heavy, and lugubrious air. The vault is supported by a single column in the middle, so thick and massive as to obstruct the view ; and the sovereign seated on his throne must be concealed by it from very many of the company The great hall in the preceptory of the Teutonic

Knights at Marienburg is on the same plan; but
how different in execution! There the roof is
formed by a group of shallow vaults all meeting in
the middle, and the support is a single granite
pillar, small, delicate, and beautiful. It is impossible to give an idea in words of the effect produced
by this union of the slender shaft with the depend-
ing vaults. The pillar is like the slight stem of
a flower, surmounted by that delicate, yet gorgeous
cup, whose lips seem to widen that they may catch
the dews of the morning as they fall; and the
waving margin of this exquisite cup is caught, as it
rises, in the circles of the arches, and mingled
inextricably with the roof.

The treasury of the Kremlin, contained in the
new arsenal, is a very remarkable and complete collection of historical objects. The portraits of the
tsars, their crowns, thrones, sceptres, globes, and
jewels, form part of this unique museum; but a
multitude of less important articles, such as canes,
goblets, paternosters, &c., which belonged to the
various princes, are likewise arranged in their res-
pective order. The whole is highly curious to the
student of historical manners.

But the grand attraction of the Kremlin is its
whole as a picture; and, united to this whole, when
standing on the esplanade, the spectator sees a
great part of the city lying at his feet. In the
annexed beautiful view, the tower of Ivan Velikoi,
and the cathedrals are in front. On the right, is a
corner of the new palace, at the window of which

Drawn by A. G. Vickers.

Engraved by H. Wallis.

Tower of Ivan Velikir.

MOSCOW.

London. Fisher & Co.

the emperor shows himself to his subjects. A crowd of figures resembling these may be seen every day on the same spot, but generally mixed with coaches and droskis.

Among the group in the foreground are itinerant venders of luxuries, not only for the populace, but, strange to say, for the rich also. I have seen ladies, waiting there in their coach and four to see the emperor on parade, purchase bread or cakes from the hawkers, and eat them with much appetite: the identical cakes having just been fingered, and pinched, and pressed to the noses of the lowest rabble before their eyes.

The other dainties exposed for sale are sausages, red-herrings, apples preserved in quass, stewed pears spitted in dozens upon a stick, nuts, oranges, dried plums, gingerbread, small rings of bread called crindles, and kalatches, a species of roll with what looks as if intended for a handle. The last-mentioned bread is peculiar to Moscow, where there are upwards of ninety establishments that bake nothing else. When the emperor presented his son, the crown prince who was born here, to the citizens, he called him " his Moscow kalatch."

There is also bleenie, carried about hot on wooden dishes, and covered with a bason. This is a kind of pancake made of buck-wheat, about the size of a saucer, and strewed with crumbs either of boiled egg or raw onions. It is eaten with hemp-oil. Another cake of a similar kind called karavai, the invention of which is due to the Tatars, is made also of buck-wheat, but in a conical form. It is cut down the middle, dipped in oil, and clapped into the mouth. We are also treated with great quantities of dried mushrooms, cooked in hemp-oil. They are of quite a different kind from the champignons, and, when well-dressed, I found them more agreeable. The Russians are great eaters of oil; but not of train-oil, or lamp-oil, as they will have it in England.

The liqueurs for the refreshment of the crowd are, in the first place, quass. This is a substitute for small beer, and is drunk even at the tables of the nobility. It is sourish but undecided, and is disagreeable to most strangers, both in taste and flavour. It is not only used as a drink, however, but as a soup. In the latter state it receives the addition of onions, leeks, &c., and is eaten with raw fish; but I once saw it enriched, also, with olives, capers—and brown sugar. On the occasion alluded to, a German lady expressed her entire satisfaction with the dish, both by words and deeds. In the former state I met with it at the tables of the first nobility. I was once betrayed into tasting it; but I think I could not "sup full of horrors" of the kind to save my life.

When quass is carried about the streets, it is either in large globular glass bottles, or in small casks. In the former it is drunk in tumblers; in the latter it is supped with a wooden spoon, which answers for a measure. There is a superior kind called kislis-chee, which is effervescent, and tolerably well-tasted, resembling something between soda water and ginger beer.

Sbeeten is made of boiling water, capsicum, honey, laurel leaves, and cloves or cinnamon; and is carried about hot in brass kettles.

Tea is also a common drink in the streets, and becoming more so every day. A porter will frequently ask for money to get a cup of tea, instead of a glass of spirits.

The only sort of spirits to be seen in the open air, is votki, commonly described as a kind of brandy, but in reality a modification of whiskey. It is distilled from grain, and is not stronger than the common gin of London. It is entirely abandoned to the common people; and I could only taste it at all, by prevailing upon Mrs. Wilson, my hostess at St. Petersburg, to send for some on purpose. It resembles whiskey disguised a little with juniper, but is much milder, and sufficiently agreeable in the taste.

Within the city of Moscow I never saw above two or three examples of intoxication, and I would say, that the lower classes of the Russians are now decidedly more sober than the English. The change also with regard to tobacco is extraordinary. In 1663-4 the author of the " Relation des Trois Ambassades," informs us that they were addicted to the use of this narcotic to a frightful degree. They smoked through a cow's horn, and so furiously that a few whiffs were sufficient to empty the bowl, when they fell to the ground in a kind of swoon.

Towards the close of the last century the habit, according to Tooke, was altogether eradicated ; and now, the only great smokers are a few of the upper classes, who perhaps at first gave themselves into the practice as a matter of fashion.

Drawn by A. G. Vickers.

Engraved by J. H. Kernot.

Printed by Jennings & Fisher.

Gate of St Nicholas.

(Wall of the old City Moscow.)

CHAPTER XIV.

Nikolskoi gate of the Kremlin—bazaar—Russian café, or tavern—public walks—baths—whether favourable or unfavourable to the health—bearded merchants—description of a grand dinner at one of their houses—apartments—salutations—dress of the company—division of the sexes—repast—toasts—kissing—adjournment to the drawing-room —merchants' wives in the summer-gardens—promenade of the Marina Rochcha—promenade of Petrovski.

THE traveller who enters the Kremlin by the Holy Gate, and makes such a tour as I have indicated by touching slightly on the more prominent objects, will find himself, after inspecting the Treasury, at the Nikolskoi gate. Annexed is an exterior view of this gate, with its beautiful Gothic tower. The latter is altogether modern, having been rebuilt after the destruction of the city in 1812; and the artist, without outraging the kind of uniformity preserved throughout the whole, has contrived to make it the most elegant of all. Above the entrance is an inscription, by which we learn that, at the great explosion, when a considerable part of the arsenal and the gate were destroyed, a lantern before the image of Saint Nicolas (seen in the engraving) had not even its glass broken.

At the bottom of the picture is the fantastic church of Vassili Blagennoi already mentioned; to the left of which lies the bazaar, one of the most enormous collection of shops in the world, from which the Kitaï-gorod, where we now are, takes its name. The bazaar is divided into twenty-five galleries, almost all devoted to the sale of some particular merchandise, and the number of shops is considerably upwards of five thousand.

The most interesting species of barter, however, goes on in the open air. Its objects are old clothes, old arms, old every thing; and the street where it is conducted resembles a fair.

Here also is the place where the merchants congregate, and where you may see all the costumes of the east mingling with those of Europe. Opposite the exchange is a café, or tavern, which the stranger should not fail to visit. The waiters are clothed in white linen from top to toe. When the guest demands a pipe, it is brought to him in the shape of a long thin branch of cherry tree, to which is affixed a small earthen bowl. The waiter always takes the trouble of lighting the pipe with his own mouth, and then hands it to his employer.

Some sit sipping tea, with their elbows planted luxuriously upon the table, and a bit of sugar in one hand, which they suck as they sip. Some call for wine, which is brought to them, as they usually desire it, in very large glasses; but others treat themselves and a friend to a bottle of Russian champagne. This excellent wine is made in the Krimea; and is sold for three rubles the bottle: but most of the upper classes, I do not know why, prefer giving twelve rubles a bottle for French champagne.

This part of the town contains also the various tribunals, and two public printing offices.

The Beloï-gorod, surrounding the Kremlin and the Kitaï-gorod except on the water side, contains the principal streets, the hotel of the governor, the bank, the university, the foundling hospital, &c. &c. The Kremlin gardens separate it from the Kremlin on the west, and form the finest promenade in this city of promenades. The place, however, is comparatively deserted. The citizens prefer walking on the open boulevards, in the midst of the noise and bustle of the street; while the nobility parade themselves in one which seems their own by patent, and where they are to be seen every evening, the ladies with a footman walking behind them, even when escorted by gentlemen.

The Kremlin gardens extend to the river, very near the Stone Bridge. This is as yet the only stone bridge in Moscow; and, therefore, it has no other name. In the opposite view it is seen from

the right bank of the river, and the buildings of the
Kremlin appear advantageously surmounting it with
their numerous spires.

A little lower down than the bridge, on the same
side as the Kremlin, is an immense bathing establishment frequented by half the population of
Moscow.

The custom of bathing has gone very much
out of fashion among the upper classes; but the
others still take a grand scrubbing every Saturday.
Each bath costs them only twelve kopeks, or little
more than a penny; but from that sum the price
ascends, for those who insist upon luxury, to five
rubles, about four shillings and two pence. These
high-priced baths, however, are of hot water; the
lower of steam. In either, an attendant is necessary
to rub the epidermis off the sufferer with birch
twigs.

It is usual for a man and his wife to go publicly
into the same bathing-room together; a custom
which of course brings the baths under suspicion as
a place of intrigue, and may probably in the end
ruin them altogether. It was this, still more than
the introduction of the use of linen, which contributed to do away with such establishments in the
rest of Europe. They became a resort for the idle
and dissipated of both sexes, who met there daily to
gossip and retail news; and at length their character
became so bad, that in many parts of France, for
instance, priests were forbidden to go near them.
When the respectable classes were thus banished, it is

Drawn by A. G. Vickers.

The Stone Bridge.
MOSCOW.

London, Published Oct 1, 1835, for the Proprietors by Longman & Co. Paternoster Row, Rittner & C.º Paris. Asher Berlin.

Engraved by J.º Cousen.

easy to see that the poor could not long maintain them; for society has little respect for things peculiar to the poor, more especially when they are of a vicious tendency.

As for the Russians, they cannot yet be said to enjoy the blessing of clean linen, and therefore they must continue yet awhile longer to boil their skins in steam and perspiration. The lower classes wear their shirt ostentatiously over their trowsers, where it hangs like a kilt; and as for the higher, including even many persons in good circumstances, I was assured that they are satisfied with a change once a month provided they have a *front* (a false collar and breast) for Sundays and holidays.

I do not think that the Russian bath, even when frequently taken, is unwholesome. I attribute the premature old age of the women entirely to the unnatural atmosphere in which they live for eight months of the year. I know one distinguished lady in Moscow who uses the bath so hot that she requires several attendants, that they may relieve one another alternately. Her daughter, on the other hand, has such a horror of this sort of parboiling, that she advised me strenuously rather to " burst in ignorance " than make the experiment. Of these two, however, the older lady is to all appearance by far the stronger and healthier.

The public baths are frequented chiefly by the peasants and the mercantile class; at least they are the resort of very few of the ladies of the higher ranks. These, generally speaking, have given up the practice of bathing altogether, or when they do continue it, as in the case of the lady alluded to above, they have the bath in their own houses.

I regret that I am unable to give all the information I could wish with regard to the customs of the merchants. Indeed, I found almost as great a difficulty in getting an introduction into the family of a real Russian as into the harem of a Turk.

The highest class of merchants have entirely laid aside their national peculiarities, and in fact are very little, if at all, distinguished from the nobles. It is the lower class—they who still rejoice in a beard and a caftan, who are the true Russians. They frequently purchase, from ostentation, the house of a nobleman; but they inhabit only the worst corner of it, retaining the rest for show.

On the occasion of a grand dinner, the guests are received in the hall by several bearded servants, and conducted into the ante-room, where cloaks and shawls are to be deposited. These servants, together with the lacqueys who wait at table, are hired for the occasion.

The next room you enter is probably the dining-room, where you see the tables spread out for the expected repast. Through this, and possibly one or two more, you are conducted into the drawing-room. It is painted a deep and bright blue colour; for this is a favourite colour with the Russians. The walls are covered with family portraits, for the merchant has begun to pique himself upon his family, and

with other large pictures, original in one sense of
the word. In a corner is the household god
decorated with ribbons, Easter-eggs, and artificial
flowers, mingled with the faded palms of the
preceding Easter tide. Before the image hangs a
lighted lamp of many-coloured glass suspended by a
brass chain.

Here are seated a party of ladies in the nervous
silence of expectation. The gentlemen as yet
arrived do not muster strong enough to attack this
citadel of beauty: we have left them caballing in
small groups in the dining-room and intermediate
rooms. Being strangers we bow profoundly; the
lady of the house graciously: but one of us, who
has the good fortune to be on more intimate terms,
steps up to where she is sitting. He salutes her
hand, and while raising his head she kisses him on the
brow; and the little ceremony strikes us as being at
once the most kindly and graceful we have ever
seen. Reassured by this transaction, and feeling a
sort of confidence that the meeting is not for the
purpose of an execution, we turn round, and bowing
several times to the fair circle, the individuals of
which all bow several times too, we stand aside to
watch the progress of events.

The company now come rapidly in, and the
malcontents in the other rooms, take the opportunity of slinking in under convoy. The ladies kiss
each other vociferously, and the gentlemen inter-hug
also, and probably kiss too, although the sound
is lost in their wilderness of beard.

The ladies are in general fashionably dressed, but somewhat overdone. This is the distinction between them and the nobility.

"Is that the Princess ———— ?" said I one day to a friend, pointing to a lady whose back was turned towards me.

"It is very like her," he replied, "but no: she is too well dressed—that must be a merchant's wife."

On the present occasion the small handkerchief which they wear on the head in the streets is in most cases laid aside, except by the older ladies. It is always of some soft indefinite hue, and is occasionally bound with a narrow gold border. The rest of their attire consists of a gown of very rich thick silk, generally of the deepest crimson, or some other flagrant colour. As for the men, they are almost all in beard, caftan, and boots, a dress which is never changed even for mourning. The few who appear "German-fashion"—that is to say, in the European pig-tail—appear beside the others the most miserable and insignificant little devils imaginable.

It is proper to say, that after the first salutations are over, the gentlemen fall back, and take up a defensive position in another part of the room; while the ladies, as if disconcerted by the prudence of the enemy, after a few faint attempts at conversation, sink again into a profound, but not tranquil silence. This is interrupted by the servants bringing in what in England would be called a "snack," or whet, consisting of caviar, anchovies, smoked salmon, salted herrings, cheese, onions, &c. &c., with small pieces of bread, and liqueurs of different sorts. The same custom prevails in the houses of the nobility. All do justice to these good things; and the ladies, invigorated by the refreshment, are able, on dinner being announced, to fall into rank, defile before the gentlemen, and march with a show of considerable firmness through the suite of rooms. The gentlemen, on their part, wait till the last rank and file have cleared the door; and then after holding a brief council, in which precedence and command are settled, follow gallantly to the field.

The dinner is absolutely the same as that which you meet with at the tables of the nobility. It is prepared by French artists hired for the occasion, and the glass, earthenware, plate, knives and forks, &c., are all obtained in the same way. The table is decorated besides with gilded temples crowned with artificial flowers, and bronze candelabras.

When the guests are seated, the two hostile lines facing each other, the master and mistress of the feast remain standing. It is their business to attend to the wants of the company themselves, and to see that the servants do their duty. Nothing can escape their observation. Your plate does not remain a moment empty, nor your glass a moment either empty or full. At length a toast is proposed. It is " the Emperor !" At that instant a door flies open, and a burst of music sweeps in from the next room, the guests joining their acclamations to the

sound.   The new national hymn follows, "God save
the Emperor !" and receives additional power from
the practised ears and voices of the company.   Other
toasts speedily follow, such as "the Ladies"—"the
Gentlemen," and are done honour to in flowing
bumpers of champagne.   Many other French wines
are on the table, as also madeira, which is much
esteemed by the Russians, and a bottle of port set
down expressly for the Englishman.

Soon, however, the wine appears to grow distasteful; and one of the company, with a knowing
look to his compeers, declares that he thinks it
wants sweetening.   At this signal the master and
mistress of the feast exchange a hearty kiss, and the
drink goes down as before.   But in a few minutes
another malcontent raises his voice, and thus the
complaint passes from one to the other—" This wine
is not sweet enough !"—the host and hostess kissing
each time, till they are ready to faint.

The lady, however, takes her revenge.   She fixes
an inveterate eye upon the glasses, which must be
emptied within a given time, and filled as soon as
emptied.   The lights at length begin to misconduct
themselves.   They twinkle, if they do not absolutely
hop.   As for you, you are no doubt deadly sober; but
willing to remain so, are desirous of making your
escape.   You seize the opportunity of the hostess's
back being turned, and vanish from the room; but
alas ! you are caught on the middle of the stairs,
and conducted back a prisoner.

At her own time she gives the signal, and all get

up from the table. The ladies must have been conquerors in the pitched battle, for in the march to the drawing-room, they again take precedence of the lords of the creation. The latter, indeed, show some little symptoms of the confusion of defeat ; but these are completely dissipated by the refreshment of a cup of coffee. In fine, the company take their leave with abundance of bows, kisses, and thanks ; and when you get into the street, instead of " Hold your tongue," to the challenge of the pole-axe man, you reply with ineffable good humour, " Go to the devil, my fine fellow !"

The merchants' wives, as I have said, rarely leave their houses, except to go to church, or to the promenade. They live in a kind of eastern seclusion, which appears to be the only remains of the frightful state of bondage to which their grandmothers were condemned. They are said to amuse themselves from morning till night with drinking tea, of which they swallow forty or fifty cups in the day. They thrive upon this beverage as the English do upon ale; for they are in general fat—which, to a Russian of this class, means beautiful.

I went to the promenade of the Summer Garden for the express purpose of seeing them collectively, and I was not disappointed. The splendour of the costume, the beauty (real and artificial) of the women, and the solemnity with which the interminable procession marched along the walks—all formed such a mixture of the odd and agreeable as I have rarely seen. They were almost all dressed in

cloaks of the richest silk, remarkable either for the
intensity or delicacy of the colour: for the time was
just midway between summer and winter, when the
hues of either season were not out of the way.
Their ear-rings were in general of pearls, and they
wore gold chains. Their complexions afforded some
of the most extraordinary specimens of painting
ever witnessed. The mechanical part was admirable,
but the design too ambitious to deceive; for a woman
with a natural face resembling many of those I saw,
would have been

        " An angel ready made for heaven !"

All seemed conscious that they were dressed and
painted to their utmost—that they were there not to
take a walk, but to form an exhibition; and the
earnest gravity with which they thus marched in
procession, looking neither to the right, nor to the
left, was the best part of the entertainment.

Another promenade, in the Marina Rochcha, or
Mary's wood, was of a different kind. Here were
assembled representatives of all the classes of society,
and the tout ensemble was the most striking that
can be imagined. Carpets were spread here and
there beneath the trees, with large brass tea-urns,
and other materials for this essential beverage.
Turks, Persians, and Tatars were squatted every
where around, intermingled with the families of the
Russian merchants. Some were walking in groups,

some playing at a kind of battledore and shuttle-cock, and some listening to the military music supplied by government. Here a troop of Gipsey girls screamed the airs of their unknown nation; there a circle of Russian lasses performed the Korovoda; and close by, three or four mujiks, surrounded by a crowd of spectators, danced a kind of hornpipe with a wildness of extacy which I have never seen equalled.

This scene was exhibited on one side of the carriage-way; while on the other there were tents, booths, taverns, with fields and groves between. The principal amusement here was a race of two men and a woman, or two women and a man, the third party endeavouring to prevent the other two from meeting. But the *business* was the sale and purchase of votki. In some tents it was distributed by wholesale only, in large square bottles; but in general it was doled out in small measures, the purchaser spilling a portion into a tub as the perquisite of the waiter.

The carriage-way was crowded with the equipages of the nobility; but at an early hour these disappeared, and left the scene of merriment to the multitude.

At the promenade of Petrovski I saw the nobles in all their glory; but the scene was not half so agreeable, or so amusing as either of the other two. The double line of carriages was immense, but most of them were untidy, and many shabby; the harness was dirty; and the horses, although frequently good, far from having the appearance of being well cared for.

In this respect the studs of the merchants are by much the best. The Cossacks on guard between the lines were mounted on horses, that in the cant language now obsolete in England, were " rum ones to look at, though good ones to go." They seemed as if they had been taken for the occasion from a little country cart after a hard day's work. Behind, on the turf, were posted at regular distances the corps de lanterne, dressed in coarse grey cloth, and looking like parish paupers. The emperor was there on horseback.

The Kremlin gardens, both within and without the walls, ought to afford a promenade every evening; but the latter especially is a complete solitude in the heart of a great city. Annexed is the view enjoyed from the declivity of the esplanade leading down into the gardens.

Drawn by A. G. Vickers.

Engraved by J. T. Willmore.

MOSCOW.

From the Esplanade of the Kremlin.

London. Published Oct.r 1.1835. for the Proprietor. by Longman & Co Paternoster Row. Rittner & Co Paris. Asher Berlin.

CHAPTER XV.

Charitable institutions—foundling hospital—crown colony—
technological school—literary education—maternity wards
—question of the morality of the institution—hospice for
widows—statistics of the Foundling—Lombard bank—
Alexandrine orphan institution—Simonov monastery—
ceremonies of the monks—nunneries—Tatar mosque—
description of the service—Russian prostrations—Tatar
prince.

THE foundation of the civil hospitals dates from
1682 ; that of the military from the time of Peter
the Great. At present, they amount in number to
seventy-one, and include by far the most splendid
houses in the city. They are in general similar to
those of St. Petersburg, which have been minutely
described by another writer ; but a few are peculiar
to Moscow.

The Foundling Hospital is one of the most stupendous institutions of charity in the world. On entering it, the stranger finds himself in a town, and yet in a single house, containing six thousand inhabitants!

The infant is received here without a single question being asked, and a number hung round its neck, a duplicate of which is given, if desired, to the person who brings it. That person, probably the mother of the child, is permitted to remain as nurse if she chooses, when she is fed and clothed at the expense of the institution, and receives fifty kopeks a day. After a certain time, the woman carries away the child to her home; or, if this is not convenient, a new nurse is provided, who takes charge of it for seven or eight years, commencing at the rate of five rubles a month. It is then brought back to the hospital, and its education begun.

When a little lad of this age discovers a natural incapacity for learning, he is sent to what are called the colonies of the crown. He does not, however, become exactly a crown-peasant, for he cannot be drawn as a recruit. At the proper period he is married to any girl he may fancy belonging to the establishment, and destined for the same way of life. Every thing requisite for the marriage is provided—a cottage, ready furnished, to receive them; a horse, a cow, a few sheep, &c. They pay no imposts, not even the capitation tax, for the first three years; but, after that, they pay as government peasants. The colony is provided with a school, a doctor, and a church ; and thus these children of shame or misery sit down in comfort for life, with every thing around them necessary for the soul or body.

The children who exhibit a turn for handicraft trades, are sent to a branch of the institution called the technicological school. Here I saw them at work according to their different tastes or ages ; the younger children busily employed at toy-making, and the others at cabinet-work, carpentry, smith-work, &c. At the dinner hour they washed and dressed, and, marching into the room in file, sat down to a comfortable meal, at which they used silver plate.

Those boys or girls who exhibit a capacity to learn are put into regular classes in the House. The boys are taught Russian, Latin, German, French, history, geography, natural philosophy, and mathematics. Some are then sent to the Academy of Medicine, where they take degrees; others to the University ; and others are entered in the body of licensed teachers. The girls, in addition to most of the above branches, learn music and dancing ; and they are then placed out as governesses. Even when they lose their situation, they still remain under the care of this extraordinary institution; and, when insulted or oppressed, they apply direct to the governor of Moscow, who acts as their guardian.

But the house extends its charity still further. It provides for the child even before its birth, by receiving the mother during her confinement. There

x

are two wards of this kind; one for indigent married women who come openly, and one for females who wish to wrap this epoch of their lives in mystery. In the latter case no question is asked: the patient may even conceal her face with a mask if she chooses.

The question of morality connected with this subject has been frequently discussed. The advocates of the Foundling Hospital say, that, even admitting its existence to increase the proportion of enfans trouvés, still the lives of an immense number must be saved by it. This becomes properly a question of statistics, and it is difficult to answer in a country like Russia. I do not think, however, that the number of infanticides is greater to any considerable degree in the provinces where no Foundling Hospital exists. Shame has rarely this effect in Russia. The dreadful mortality among the young children of the peasantry still goes on, and it proceeds principally from neglect.

" God will take care of my child," says the mujik's wife, " if it is his will that it should live ;" and, laying it down in its cradle to be swung by the angels, she goes out to her labour in the fields. This is the true reason why the Russian peasantry are so strong and healthy; for, in reality, only those gifted by nature with an iron constitution survive the tender years of infancy. Among persons of this class, three children are considered a large family ; while double, and sometimes treble the number, grace the board of the nobility. But, if the peasant woman is careless of her offspring, she is, in like manner, careless of herself; and both are equally fatal to the child. The next day after the infant is born, she resumes her work in the fields as if nothing had happened, and is thus often rendered incapable of acting the part of a nurse.

In the secret maternity ward there are two thousand cases every year, while in the public one there are only fifty.

There is, also, connected with the Foundling Hospital, a hospice for the widows of civil or military officers. They retain their children till the age of eight years for the boys, and eleven for the girls; when they are put, at the expense of the institution, into the proper seminaries of education. Some of these widows take the oaths as Sisters of Charity, and devote their lives to the duty of rendering gratuitous assistance to the sick.

The Foundling Hospital was founded by the Empress Catharine II. in 1764, and opened on her birthday, the twenty-first of April. The first child was christened Catharine, and the second, Paul. In that year, 523 children were received; in 1834, 8312. The following is a classified table of the number under the care of the institution on the day of my visit.

	Males.	Females.
Grown-up children, including those in the classes . .	432	445
Midwifery Students . .		48

	Males.	Females.
Children at the breast	299	357
At widows' alms-houses	34	51
Under the parents' care	1691	1492
In the infirmary	19	38
At nurse in the villages	10781	13579
Colony at Seratoff	412	411
At the Technicological School	196	
In sundry places	106	60

13,970 16,481

Total 30,451

The funds of this vast establishment are provided and managed by the Lombard Bank; an institution which receives deposits of money at five per cent, and lends on personal and other property at six per cent. It enjoys a tithe of the gross receipts of the theatre, and other public places of amusement, besides a variety of other bonuses; and its revenue is much more than sufficient to clear the expenses of the Foundling Hospital.

Independently of the branches I have mentioned, there is the Alexandrine Orphan Institution, which derives its funds from the Foundling Hospital. It was founded in 1831, under the auspices of the empress, for the orphans of individuals who had died of the cholera. It is now, however, thrown open, and receives one hundred and fifty boys, and one hundred and fifty girls, the orphans of civil and military officers.

Drawn by A. G. Vickers.

Engraved by J. T. Willmore

Printed by McQueen & Son

The Kremlin.

From the Dogg. Moscow.

London. Published Oct.¹ 1,1835. for the Proprietor. by Longman &.C.º Paternoster Row. Rittner & C.º Paris. Asher Berlin.

The boys who are educated here will go to the university attended by a tutor; and the girls, after receiving the education of accomplished women, will themselves become governesses in distinguished families, instead of the English, German, and French ladies at present employed. I never witnessed more apparent happiness than in this establishment. The gymnastic exercises of the boys would have attracted applause if performed on the stage. The air and manners of the girls had much of the ton of good society. They will speedily be removed into a new house, which has been built for their reception, near the hotel of the governor of the institution, prince Serge Gagarin.

Among the sights of Moscow, the Simonov monastery is one which the stranger should not neglect to see. It is near the farthest rampart of the city to the south; and, supposing the visitor to set out from the Kremlin, I advise him to turn round as he traverses the quay, and indulge himself with the superb view which is so happily imitated in the opposite engraving.

As we recede from the centre of the town, the houses become more enclosed in groves and gardens; and, from every little eminence we ascend, the domes and cupolas of innumerable churches are seen rising from the centre of the foliage. The Simonov monastery is enclosed within a lofty wall, through the narrow slits of which some small cannon peep at the visitor. It contains five churches, the most ancient of which dates from 1405. The ikonastas of the principal church is one of the most magnificent in Moscow. It is one mass of gilded sculpture rising to the vault, and many of the images are adorned with precious stones.

The view from the summit of the tower, however, is still better. The whole of Moscow lies before you, and the town seems to be forcing itself out into the retreating woods.

After enjoying this spectacle for some time, the bell gave notice that service was about to begin; and then came on the principal scene of the piece. The ceremonies were too numerous and complicated for description; but, every now and then, the picture formed by the monks was prodigiously fine. This was more particularly the case when they formed a hollow square in the middle of the church, with tall candlesticks before them. The light playing upon the pale face and remarkable head of one of them, in particular, would have been worth any thing to a painter.

Even here, however, among these spouseless, and, it is to be hoped, loveless, brethren, I observed the evident presence of personal vanity. The monk whose duty it was to hold a book before the superior, with a lighted candle, and whose head was thus more fully brought out, chanced to be an extremely handsome man. Instead of allowing his beard, therefore, to grow like those of the others, concealing the mouth, he had trimmed it coquettishly, twisting the upper part into military moustaches,

and leaving a tuft of hair under the lower lip
to mingle with the rest of the beard beneath.

He whose pale face and remarkable head I
observed, has done more for the monastery than
merely contributing to form the picture. He has
introduced here a style of singing which it would
be in vain to attempt to describe. It is so low,
so sweet, so rich, and yet so lofty, that if heard
even in a theatre it could not fail to excite the
deepest feelings of devotion.

The audience on this occasion consisted of many
of the upper classes; the ladies of whom, without
having any pretensions to beauty, possessed that
charming harmony of feature and expression which
is hardly any where more common than in Moscow.

The Simonov monastery may be taken as a sample,
although a favourable one, of the monastic establishments of Moscow, the rest of which I have no
space even to name. Some of the nunneries, also,
in the busier quarters of the city, are well worth
visiting. The lady abbess sailing in, and seating
herself on a kind of throne, and the sisters marching
two by two, and bowing profoundly at her footstool,
produce a scenic effect which will please the lover
of the picturesque.

The Tatar mosque is in a part of the town to
which the Tatars were formerly restricted. It is a
very plain and unstuccoed brick building. The
mezzuin did not ascend the tower, but mounted
upon a wall which overlooked the garden, where
many of the congregation were meditating, or

washing, preparatory to entering the church. His voice, as he gave out the invitation to true believers, in recitative, was extremely pleasing; and, in the midst of the profound tranquillity of the place and time, was something more.

The interior of the mosque was quite as plain as the exterior. The floor was covered, excepting the space near the door, beyond which heretics are not allowed to advance, with pieces of carpeting; and at the further end appeared an empty vaulted recess, somewhat like a fire-place. As the worshippers came in, they pulled off their shoes, "for the place is holy," unloosed a part of their turbans, and, putting both hands for a few moments to the sides of the head, in order to exclude the world, began to bow and fall on their faces like the Russians. The latter, however, are infinitely more graceful. Theirs is a true prostration; for, sinking upon their knees, they "fall all along upon the earth." The Tatars, on the contrary, sit upon their heels, and make their heads touch the ground as near their feet as possible—the opposite end of the body, of course, elevating itself in a presumptuous, if not indecorous manner.

After these genuflexions and prostrations had gone on for some time in profound silence, the mezzuin said something in a low voice; and the priest, dressed in a white turban, ascended a sort of arm chair elevated on steps, and delivered an address in recitative. He then came down, and having placed himself on his heels in his original position, looking into the vault, the congregation advanced, and formed themselves into regular lines behind him. All was death-like silence for a considerable time, till at length he spoke. At a certain word the people touched the ground with their foreheads, and rose again, all performing the ceremony with the nicest precision at one instant. This was repeated several times at long intervals, the devotees occasionally stroking their faces, which I understood was to imitate the motion of washing. They then, as if by word of command, turned their faces first to the right and then to the left, and rose up. The priest now turned round with his face towards the audience, and prayed, making use of beads like the Catholics, while the same prostrations went on as before. He then took up the Koran, and having read aloud a portion, the service of the day was over.

Among the audience there was a splendid old man, a Tatar prince, known to an English gentleman who accompanied me. To this gentleman, Mr. R——— of Moscow, whose loss of nearly a million of rubles by the French invasion has not damped his affection for his adopted country, I owe the warmest acknowledgments for a series of services as valuable as they were unmerited.

CHAPTER XVI.

Amusements of Moscow—funerals—ceremonies and processions—singular demonstrations of grief of a Russian lady for the loss of her son—Yalomensk, or the accacia palace —Catharine's country-house—Tsaritzena, or the coffin-palace—Yassenova—peasantry—remarks on the subject of their emancipation—sagacious policy of the emperor.

THERE are few public amusements in Moscow. The theatre is a colossal building, not exceeded in size, I should think, even by that of Milan. It is chiefly distinguished by its national ballets; but these were over for the season before my arrival. M. Z——, however, the director-general, a literary man of celebrity, was kind enough to give me the use of his box during my stay.

In the evening the stranger, if respectably introduced, has the choice of numerous soirées to pass
the time ; and as he will rarely dine at home, there
is abundance of variety in his recreations. Owing
to the early hour of dinner—three o'clock—the
guests retire in time either to pay visits themselves
or allow their entertainers to do so. Forenoon calls
are not in vogue, although the Muscovites are
early risers. I have myself been received by ladies
of distinction as early as ten o'clock in the morning.

Still even the forenoon will not hang heavily
upon the hands of any idler who has eyes and
imagination. The streets are an unfailing source
of amusement. Sometimes a funeral sweeps by
(if that can be called an amusement) preceded at
a great distance, and at long intervals, by men in
black, with broad brimmed hats slouching upon
their shoulders, who light the way of the cortege
with torches even at noon day. The hearse is an
open car covered by a dais, showing the lofty coffin
and its pall. The mourners follow in all sorts of
carriages, among which on one occasion I observed
several hundred droskis.

Some ecclesiastical ceremony is always going on.
You see, perhaps, a number of horses ranged round
the church, and the priests busy in sprinkling them
with holy water, and making the sign of the cross.
This cures them of restiveness, and brings them
under religious subjection to their owner. The hay
which they are to eat is blessed in like manner.
The benediction of apples is apparently more profi-

table to the priest, for he takes one out of every parcel as his own perquisite.

The processions are sometimes very magnificent. I have seen between three and four hundred priests at one time, all dressed in cloth of silver embroidered with gold, marching along with their flags and banners displayed, and thundering forth a hymn. In the opposite view of the gate of Vladimir at the southern angle of the Kitaï-gorod, one of these processions is finely introduced.

Even if the fund of interest should fail within the city, the traveller will find an inexhaustless store in the environs. The palaces, gardens, monasteries, country seats of the nobility, for a hundred miles round, offer a perpetual variety. I was invited to the consecration of a church eighty or ninety versts distant, and the lady who did me the favour, was even kind enough to send horses for me; but in consequence of some unfortunate equivoque I had otherwise disposed of myself. I regretted this much, for the circumstances had in them not a little of the strange and romantic.

The lady was born Countess Orloff, and is a niece of the famous Prince Gregory Orloff, who is supposed to have been privately married to the Empress Catharine II. She married, contrary to the wish of her family, a nobleman of rank inferior to her own, by whom she had one child, a son. This boy grew up every thing that a parent could wish. Brave, handsome, generous, of the highest blood of the country, and the heir of immense

Drawn by A. G. Vickers.

The Herman Square
MOSCOW.

Engraved by J. Carter.

London, Oct 1, 1835. Published for the Proprietor, by Longman & Co. Paternoster Row, Hinton & Co. Paris, & Asher, Berlin.

wealth, he was beloved, or flattered, by all—but he was the idol of his mother.

In due time the young man loved; but the lady, although the daughter of a nobleman high in the army, was not considered a match for him. The mother whose maternal pride and ambition were thus menaced, was thrown into consternation. She begged, prayed, threatened—all in vain: the youth was firm. She at length yielded: for he was her son, her only child, the one being in whom her hopes, her affections, her life were centred.

But during the struggle, his determination had survived his constancy. His mother's tears, expostulations, and reasonings—perhaps his more intimate acquaintance with the object of his attachment— perhaps even the jeers of his comrades, who laughed at her name Prescovia, so vulgar in Russia—perhaps all together had conspired to change his heart. At any rate, the difficulties in the way of the match were no sooner removed, than he declared suddenly that it was not his intention to marry.

The young lady had three brothers, and the consequences may be foreseen. They declared that he must either marry their sister, or fight them all three, one after another. This only served to relieve his heart, and to ennoble his cause. He met the eldest brother; they fought near St. Petersburg —and were both killed: the unhappy youth crying with his last breath, " My poor mother!"

This was ten years ago. Since that period the mother has devoted her life to mourning. A church is now rising on the spot where her son fell; and another at her own house at Otrada, to the consecration of which I was invited, has been completed. In the vaults of the monastery of Novospaskoi a splendid monument has been erected to his memory, where the commemorative service is performed by the monks four times a week, and where a lamp is kept perpetually burning beside the tomb. When going to pray there herself, his favourite horse accompanies her, and on their return she feeds the animal with white bread with her own hand. At the anniversary of the fatal duel, she shuts herself up from the world for some weeks, with the portrait, clothes, &c., of her dead son arranged before her. She loads every one with gifts and charities who chooses to claim acquaintance with him however slight. To this hour she is in deep mourning.

Owing to the equivoque I have alluded to, instead of taking a part in the mournful solemnities of Otrada, I rode out into the country with a friend, Mr. H————, to whose kind attentions, as well as to his intimate knowledge of the Russian language, I am indebted for much both of the useful and agreeable.

We first went to see the palace of Yalomensk built by Alexis, father of Peter the Great. This edifice, however, is now among the things that were; and we saw only a very fine acacia hedge, planted upon the foundations in such a manner as to describe minutely the plan of the building. In front is a large stone on which, tradition says, the people placed their petitions; and at a short distance the tree, surrounded by a table and benches, under which young Peter received his lessons. This tree, which in England would be considered one of very ordinary size, is here reckoned a giant.

We had approached the acacia palace by an avenue, the gate of which presented something curious. It was an arched building, surmounted by an onion-shaped dome cut vertically down the middle, so as to expose a flat surface. At the middle of the avenue, a little way to one side, was the site of the palace; and at the opposite end, an edifice, traversed by arched gateways, which served as the offices. Beyond this, on the right hand is a church, and on the left a country-house built by Catharine II. The latter possesses one large hall, but the other apartments are extremely mean. The view, however, from the tower, which commands a considerable space, is truly imperial.

Returning to the highway, from which we had diverged, and pursuing our ride, we reached Tsaritzena, about fourteen versts from the city barriers. This palace was never completed, and never inhabited, and yet it is now a ruin. Catharine, for whom it was built by Potemkin, on seeing it for the first time thought it looked like a hearse, and turned back in consternation. Her idea was perfectly just; for in fact even when standing close by, the roof resembles the lofty lid of a Russian coffin, and the small towers may very well be taken for the ornaments of the bier. Surrounding the palace is a perfect wilderness of walks and gardens, where the citizens of Moscow delight to wander, sometimes passing the whole summer's night in little pavilions that are placed here and there throughout.

From Tsaritzena we crossed the country to Yassenova, the seat of Prince G————; where, although his excellency was unwell, we received a hospitable welcome from the princess—not to talk of a luxurious dinner, served under orange and lemon trees, and other exotic plants. The prince is a great breeder of merino sheep, and his wool this year was thought to be the best in the exposition. I had much pleasure in viewing his flock, and the excellent appointments of the place in which they are kept; but still more in visiting the peasantry of his village, and inquiring personally, with Mr. H———— for my interpreter, into their domestic arrangements and general situation.

I found them as happy and comfortable as any peasantry in the world, with large gardens well stocked with fruit trees, and their public bath—an unfailing sign in Russia—clean and in good order. The very reverse of this description, however, applied to a village close by, of which the proprietor was a lady. This is the dreadful evil of the system. The happiness or misery of a great portion of the people of Russia depends upon the moral character of comparatively a small number of individuals.

The late emperor Alexander was the most

enlightened friend the peasantry have yet had; and from the conspicuous energy and intelligence of Nicolas still more may be expected. But it is mere childishness to deny that the subject is invested with great difficulty. The emperor feels more acutely than any man in the state, that the great mass of a people coming every day nearer in contact with the civilized nations of Europe cannot long remain in this condition; and what is more to the purpose when talking of a sovereign, he feels that it is not his interest that they should do so. The manner of their emancipation, however, has become a question of much intricacy, and in the present wretched state of the administration of the laws it seems almost impossible to attain the object.

The public of England, perhaps, will be surprised to learn, that independently of the opposition such a measure would receive from some of the landholders, it would be opposed by a great body of the peasants themselves. The Russian peasant, generally speaking, has no idea of liberty in the abstract—he does not wish to be free merely for the sake of freedom. If a noble gives his serf liberty, he of course resumes his land. " But the land is *mine!*" cries the serf, " it has come down to me from my ancestors—it is there where my father was buried, and where my young ones were born!" To become a tenant, liable to be turned off at legal warning, instead of a feudal vassal holding his lands on the bond of fidelity, does not appear liberty to him. If he forms an idea of the word at all, it is that he may still retain his land, and yet not pay the landlord.

Again, when the Russian landlord resumes his land he will of course rescind all the privileges which time and custom have secured to the peasants; and I should like to see the stare of the latter when told for the first time, that they were henceforth to have no property in the fish of the river or the fowls of the air!

I have said that the measure of emancipation would be opposed only by some of the nobles. Many, on the other hand, would give it their zealous support. When a change of proprietors takes place, it is usual for the peasants, uncertain of the character of their new master, to *beg* their liberty; and many of them obtain it. A lady, whose acquaintance I had the honour of making at Moscow, Mademoiselle D——f, one of the most intelligent women in the empire, lately bought an estate of five hundred peasants. Immediately on her arrival a few of them begged and obtained their liberty; but although she proclaimed throughout the property that all who asked should receive the boon without money and without price, not a single application was afterwards made. Another acquaintance, M. Z—— of Moscow, on coming into possession of a small village of forty or fifty males, called them all about him, and offered them their freedom, with the liberty of remaining upon the land as tenants. They all refused.

On the other hand, the peasants who have

obtained by purchase, or otherwise, the permission of their lord to reside in towns, necessarily acquire the common feelings of civilization, and learn to enter into the ideas of freemen. They regard their village comrades, however ancestral prejudice may disguise the matter, as nothing more than the slaves of the soil; and they look with a shudder upon the indignities to which they see them exposed when they happen to have either a fool or a brute for their master. These men no sooner acquire money enough, than they hasten to buy their freedom; and if they effect this (which the pride or caprice of some masters prevents), they see at once open to them the career of ambition, leading to the very highest offices of the state.

The present emperor has taken this class of freemen under his special protection. He has ennobled, as it were, the body, and made it a mark for general ambition. He is sagacious enough to see that by such measures he makes himself be looked upon as a good angel by the mujiks. It matters not what is their situation. However sore may be their thraldom when in the hands of a tyrannical master, it is not the government that is to blame. Although occasionally (and it happened twice during my sojourn in Moscow) they assassinate their tyrant, they are always ready to lay down their lives for the emperor.

CHAPTER XVII.

Departure of the exiles for Siberia—distribution of kalatches
—Dr. Haas—singular scene in the Ostrog—police—story
of its absurd severity—curious anecdote—the evil eye—
education and character of the upper classes—English in
Moscow—their church—funeral of an English lady—
climate—cheapness of living—population statistics—adieu
to the Holy City.

The departure of the exiles for Siberia is a scene
which should not be missed by the traveller: but in
order to let him enjoy it at his ease, one thing is
necessary to be understood. The mere fact of trans-
portation is not looked upon as a severe punishment;
for the great body of the criminals consists of persons
who have been accustomed all their lives to a compulsory servitude, as severe as that which awaits
them beyond the Ural mountains. Condemnation

to the *mines* in Siberia is what they dread—and
with great justice; for this is a substitution for
capital punishment, and answers the same purpose,
only extending the time occupied by the act of dying
from a few minutes to a few years.

In a temporary depôt, erected on the summit of
the Sparrow hills, I found the destined wretches
about to commence their march. A long chain secured both legs at the ancles, and, to prevent it from
incommoding them in walking, was fastened to
their belt, or sash. A great many were Jews, most
of them mujiks; and all, with the exception of one
man, were free from those physiognomical marks of
atrocity which are commonly supposed to distinguish
the guilty. Some carts were near, filled with their
wives and children, and some of their male relations
stood beside them unmanacled, who had likewise
petitioned to be permitted to share their exile.

In the middle stood a man who had a good deal
of the air of an English dissenting clergyman; but
the shape of his clothes and hat, and the large
buckles in his shoes, seemed to belong to the fashion
of an earlier day. His appearance inspired me with
instinctive respect, and his face seemed absolutely to
beam with the purest and noblest philanthropy. He
was occupied in distributing moral and religious
books to such of the prisoners as could read, and in
hearing patiently, and often redressing instantly,
their complaints. The exiles, on their part, seemed
to look upon him as a friend—a father; but their
affection was mingled with the deepest respect.

Many prostrated themselves at his feet, as before a holy image, and touched the ground with their forehead. On taking leave, he embraced and kissed them all, one by one; and the rattle of their chains, as they began the march, was mingled with sobs and blessings.

The cortege, however, had hardly began to move, when it was stopped by the appearance of a bearded merchant, who entered the prison hastily, followed by servants bearing large baskets of kalatches. This is a species of charity very common in Moscow. Fine bread is distributed in the prisons almost daily; and, on the present occasion, all the exiles and their families received one or more large rolls.

Dr. Haas, for this is the philanthropist's name, is in a kind of official situation, acting as the secretary of a charitable body; and he passes his life among the sick and the captives, in the double capacity of physician to the soul and body. He told me various interesting anecdotes of the prisoners, which I regret I have not space to repeat; and showed me, with a delightful pride, the hospital attached to the depôt, where many poor wretches who had never before in their lives known the luxury of a bed, were lying in as much external comfort as if they had been the first nobles in the land.

I went afterwards to the Ostrog, the principal prison of the town, in which the classification of the prisoners is strictly attended to. This, however, is all I can say in its favour; the buildings being sin-

gularly mean, and the walls of the apartments dirty.
Here, however, I again met Dr. Haas, the guardian
genius of the scene—and in rather an odd predicament.

A sick prisoner, it seems, had longed for a cup of
sbeeten, and the doctor had promised it. His
assistant, however, although furnished with the
necessary directions, had neglected to fulfil the
promise; but, when reminded of it by the poor
man, he desired another to do so—and that other
was prevented, by being taken ill himself. The
invalid hereupon becoming desperate, complained to
the doctor; and the doctor, full of indignation,
declared that he who had been guilty of breaking
the promise should present the cup upon his knees.
The affair was at this point when I arrived. The
third party to the transgression could not, and the
assistant would not, kneel; and Dr. Haas, surrounded by a group of turnkeys and felons, was
about to go upon his knees to present a cup of
sbeeten to the sick prisoner! The reader, no doubt,
will be happy to learn that he suffered himself to be
dissuaded, and that the ceremony was eventually
performed by the assistant.

The police of Moscow is very efficient; but,
as is the case in all the executive departments
of the law throughout the country, is very
unequal and capricious in its operation. I happened to become acquainted with a curious case
of absurd severity. At a time when incendi-
arism was frequent in the city, a servant-girl

found in the street a letter in which a neighbour was threatened with having his house burned down that very night. She instantly flew to the devoted family to give the alarm; and, after relating the story to her master, went to bed in a state of dreadful agitation. In the middle of a cold and stormy night, she was taken out of bed by the police, having only time to snatch up a petticoat and wrap it round her shoulders; she was dragged to the office, and, without a word of examination, knouted severely; and then thrust into prison, where she was kept for two days without food! Her crime was having warned the intended victims, instead of carrying the letter to the police; and, having been delivered of a child only a day or two before, her death from exhaustion would, in all probability, have been the consequence, had she not purchased from one of the men, for an eighty kopek piece, a small morsel of black bread.

In consequence of the severity of the police, not only to suspected criminals, but to witnesses, a Russian will never have any thing to do with a dead body which has not died in its bed. If he meets with one in the fields, or on the highway, he takes to flight as if he were afraid of the ghost. They are very attentive to the sick; but when once the breath is out, "there's an end." A friend of mine riding one day near the Simonov monastery, saw a man at a distance climb up a tree and hang himself. He immediately galloped with all his might towards the scene of action; but, before arriving, a soldier was already there from the barracks close by. This man would neither interfere himself, nor permit my friend to do so. He stood on guard very quietly till the police came up, with an immense crowd at their heels; and the first thing thought of, after taking down the body, was to fell the tree with their hatchets as being *unclean*.

This is the more curious as the general belief is, that the soul does not get clear off from the body till the ninth day after death. But the superstitions of the Russians would require a volume to themselves; and I shall only mention that the Evil Eye is the most common one in Moscow. A friend's child was taken ill in consequence of this malign, but unintentional influence; and the nurse immediately rubbed its back with the cloths that had been used at its birth. She washed the infant every night, licking its back, and spitting three times.

I need hardly say, that the higher ranks are as rarely infected with such superstitions as those of our own country.

Among persons in that class of society at Moscow, there is in general still more of warmth and kindness of manner than at St. Petersburg. Their education is good, but their reading very superficial. A traveller, in 1784, says that French and a little geography were all that was thought requisite; whereas, at present, their studies embrace French, German, and English, as well as the other branches of a polite education. I know at least half a dozen ladies who have never been out of Russia, but who

z

speak English without the slightest tinge of a foreign accent.

The number of English here is not considerable, and the great majority consists of the families of manufacturers. They have a very neat church, notwithstanding; where I heard, not without emotion, a congregation of my countrymen offering up their prayers from the centre of Russia in behalf of their native land, and their native king. On one occasion the sermon was peculiarly affecting. It was preached on the death of Mrs. F——, a beautiful, amiable, and highly-gifted young lady; whom, although expected by her in life, I was too late to see except in her coffin. At the funeral itself, my worthy friend,—if he will permit me to call him so, —the excellent and talented minister of the congregation, was so much overcome by emotion that the words of the beautiful service came only in choked and broken fragments from his lips. It was a scene I shall not readily forget—that small group of English in a lonely churchyard, weeping over the grave of their countrywoman in a foreign land.

The climate of Moscow is healthy, partly owing, no doubt, to its elevated situation, and partly to the freedom with which the wind is able to sweep between the lines of low houses. According to the hospital reports, March and October are the most fatal months for all diseases, except typhus, whose reign is in January.

The prices of the necessaries of life are low; meat being about three pence an English pound, and

Drawn by A. G. Vickers.

View of the Kremlin

From the right bank of the Moskva, Moscow

Engraved by E. Radclyffe.

Printed by McQueen & Co.

London, Published Oct.r 1 1835, for the Proprietor by Longman, & Co. Paternoster Row, Fisher & Co. Paris, & Asher Berlin.

flour not more than a halfpenny. The inhabitants, notwithstanding, complain; such rates being enormously high, compared with those of preceding years.

The population by a late census amounts to 315,152 souls. Of this number, only about a seventeenth part is noble; while more than one half is composed of peasants. The following table, without taking up much room, will give an idea of the city as it is, in the various establishments, both spiritual and corporeal, in operation for the benefit of its inhabitants.

Churches	273
Convents	21
Hospitals	71
Auberges	507
Beer retail shops	279
Bakehouses	181
Kalatch bakehouses	91
Eating-houses	170
Public Baths	37
Houses	9904
Shops	7566
Lamps	7598

I am far from flattering myself that in the foregoing pages I have been able to give a proper picture either of St. Petersburg or Moscow. If such an idea ever entered my head, it would be immediately turned out again, were it only by a sight of the large quantity of materials still lying in my portfolio untouched. In the small space, however, in which I am " cabined—cribbed—confined," I have endeavoured to touch upon those prominent points which form the outlines of the piece ; and I thus hope that I may have enabled the reader to imagine, with tolerable accuracy, the effect of the whole.

I have only to add, that after a residence of six weeks, I assumed once more the pilgrim's staff. On the opposite page the reader will take a parting glimpse, as I did, of the glories of the Kremlin from the right bank of the Moskva ; although he cannot be expected, like me, to turn his back with admiration and regret upon the HOLY CITY.

Printed by John Haddon and Co., Doctors' Commons.